Board Membe

In 2020, the COVID-19 pandemic delivered the greatest shock to the global economy since World War II. Entire societies have been locked down, and people everywhere have had to adjust to new ways of working, studying, socializing, and entertaining themselves. Notwithstanding these measures, more than 1.5 million people have died, and unemployment, inequality, and poverty have soared to new heights.

THE GLOBALIZED ECONOMY, A LIFELINE to billions of people in recent decades, has suddenly become a source of vulnerability, owing to the disruption of far-flung supply chains and governments' efforts to protect national markets. The pandemic thus has accelerated a process of deglobalization that was already underway (as reflected in plummeting world trade), and exposed deep disparities in the quality of governance across different countries and locales.

Brazil, India, the United Kingdom, and the United States – all countries with populist leaders – have performed far worse than countries like Germany, the Nordics, Japan, South Korea, and even developing countries such as Rwanda and Vietnam. By disparaging scientists and politicizing expertise, leaders like US President Donald Trump, Brazilian President Jair Bolsonaro, and Indian Prime Minister Narendra Modi have left their countries deeply polarized and tragically ill-equipped to manage a major public-health crisis and its economic fallout.

Given the pandemic's persistence, the prospects for recovery in 2021 will depend largely on how quickly vaccines are distributed worldwide. That effort could reinvigorate existing institutions of international cooperation and catalyze the establishment of new ones, and one hopes that the new US administration under President Joe Biden will push things in that direction. Whatever form it takes, robust multilateralism will be necessary both to mitigate the sharp increase in poverty and inequality caused by the pandemic, and to address longer-term challenges, particularly the existential and increasingly urgent threat posed by climate change.

The pandemic has shown how dangerous it is to ignore the warnings from science. Failing to prepare for known risks can all too easily lead to untold and unnecessary costs in human lives and livelihoods. But the crisis has also illustrated the value of working together across borders and sectors, just as it has shown us that radical changes in "business as usual" are still possible. Surprisingly for some, we have learned that leaders who dare to lead and make difficult yet responsible choices actually gain citizens' respect.

We should take all of these lessons with us into 2021. We all heard the global wake-up call in 2020. Now we must start building a more resilient society – one built on the principles of sustainability and social justice. In *The Pandemic of Fear*, political leaders, senior policymakers, and renowned scholars provide original and sharp insights into the challenges that lie ahead, both at the national and international levels. The pandemic has given us a chance to reconsider, rethink, and reform. Most important, it has renewed the demand for honest, fact-based, expert analysis in a world beset by anxiety and uncertainty.

Let 2021 mark a new dawn of reason, progress, and hope. ⬛

Connie Hedegaard served as European Commissioner for Climate Action from 2010 to 2014, and as Denmark's Minister for the Environment from 2004 to 2007 and Minister for Climate and Energy from 2007 to 2009.

PS.The Year Ahead

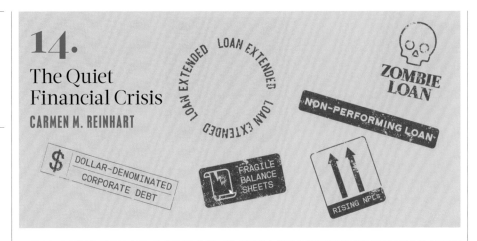

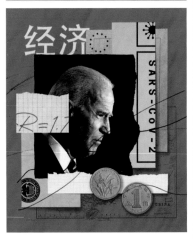

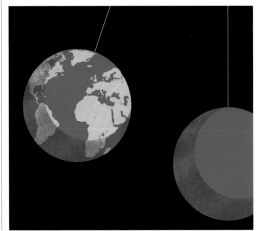

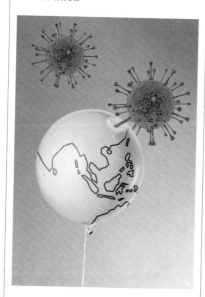

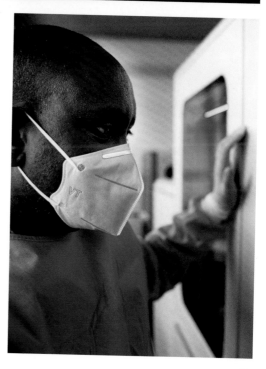

PS. The Year Ahead

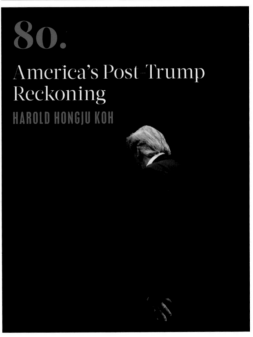

Project Syndicate

IVAN KRASTEV

*Chairman of the Center
for Liberal Strategies*

"The first thing that plague brought to our town was exile," notes the narrator in Albert Camus's *The Plague.* These days, we have an acute sense of what he meant. A society in quarantine is literally a "closed society" in which everyone but essential workers puts his or her life on hold. When people are isolated in their homes and haunted by fear, boredom, and paranoia, one of the few activities that does not cease is discussion of the virus and how it might transform the world of tomorrow. ▶

The Pandemic

IN THIS NEW WORLD, MANY governments (benevolent or otherwise) closely follow where we go and whom we meet, out of a determination to protect us from our own recklessness and that of our fellow citizens. Contact with other people has become a threat to one's existence. In many countries, unsanctioned walks in the park can elicit fines or even jail time, and unsolicited physical contact has become tantamount to a kind of societal betrayal.

As Camus observed, a plague erases the "uniqueness of each man's life" as it heightens each person's awareness of his vulnerability and powerlessness to plan for the future. It is as if Death has moved in next door. After an epidemic, everyone living can claim the title of "survivor."

But for how long will the memory of our own plague last? Could it be that in just few years we will remember it as a kind of mass hallucination caused by "a shortage of space made up for by a surplus of time," as the poet Joseph Brodsky once described a prisoner's existence?

In her marvelous book *Pale Rider*, the science writer Laura Spinney shows that the 1918-20 Spanish flu pandemic was the most tragic event of the twentieth century, at least in terms of loss of life from a single cause. The death toll surpassed that of both World War I and World War II, and may even have killed as many people as both of them combined. Yet, as Spinney notes, "When asked what was the biggest disaster of the twentieth century, almost nobody answers the Spanish flu."

More surprisingly, even historians seem to have forgotten the tragedy. In 2017, WorldCat, the world's largest library catalogue, listed roughly 80,000 books on WWI (in more than 40 languages), but barely 400 on the Spanish flu (in five languages). How can it be that an epidemic that killed at least five times as many people as WWI has resulted in 200 times fewer books? Why do we remember wars and revolutions but forget pandemics, which affect our economies, politics, and societies just as fundamentally?

Spinney's answer is that it is difficult to turn a pandemic into a compelling story between good and evil. Lacking a plot or an overarching moral,

epidemics are like Netflix series where the end of one season merely serves as a hiatus before the start of the next. The pandemic experience is one in which everything changes but nothing happens. We are asked to preserve human civilization by staying home and washing our hands. As in a modernist novel, all of the action occurs in the mind of the narrator. In my own account of the COVID-19 era, the only memorable physical objects will be the plane tickets that were never used and the face masks that were used over and over again.

And yet, the moment one goes out into the street, one realizes how much has changed. Like many of my favorite coffee shops in Vienna and Sofia, my favorite bookstore in Washington, DC, has closed. Like a neutron bomb, COVID-19 is destroying our way of life without actually damaging our material world. For much of 2020, airports were some of the saddest places on Earth – empty, silent, with only a few passengers roaming the terminals like ghosts. The increased freedom of movement over the last three decades – the ease with which people from different social classes intermingled – had become a powerful symbol of globalization. Now, that freedom has been consigned to history – or at least put on hold indefinitely.

Meanwhile, all of the public messages urging people to stay at home have prompted metaphysical reflection. Home is where one wants to be when confronted with a grave danger. When my family and I realized that we were facing a prolonged period of social distancing, we surprised ourselves by deciding to return to Bulgaria.

This was not exactly a rational decision. We have lived and worked in Vienna for a decade, we love the city, and the Austrian health-care system is far more reliable than Bulgaria's. What brought us back to Bulgaria was the understanding that we should "stay at home." Home, for us, means Bulgaria. In a time of crisis, we wanted to be closer to the people and places that we have known all our lives. We weren't alone: 200,000 Bulgarians living abroad did the same thing.

Just as many people have sought shelter in their home countries, so have they found solace in their native languages. In moments of great peril, we almost unconsciously speak in our mother tongue. In my own childhood in Bulgaria, I learned a valuable lesson from watching Soviet films about WWII. One of the most dangerous moments for Soviet female spies in Hitler's Reich was childbirth, because they would involuntarily cry out in their native Russian. Staying home meant staying in your mother tongue – and staying safe.

It is one of the great optical illusions of twenty-first-century globalization that only mobile, jet-set people are truly cosmopolitan, and that only those who feel at home in different places can maintain a universalist perspective. After all, the canonical cosmopolitan, Immanuel Kant, never left his hometown of Königsberg, which itself belonged to different empires at different times. Kant embodied the same paradox as COVID-19, which has made the world more global even as it has turned nation-states against globalization.

For example, "self-isolation" and "social distancing" have opened the European mind. Closing the borders between EU member states and locking people in their apartments has made us more cosmopolitan than ever. For those with access to

> "It might be a passing historical moment, but we cannot deny that we have come to understand what it feels like to live in one world."

communications technology, the pandemic has ushered in not de-globalization but de-localization. Our geographical neighbors are effectively no closer than our friends and colleagues abroad; we feel closer to the TV announcers than to the people down the street.

For perhaps the first time in history, people have been having the same conversations about the same topics. We have all shared the same fear. By staying at home and spending countless hours in front of screens, people have witnessed the similarities between their own experiences and those of everyone else. It might be a passing historical moment, but we cannot deny that we have come to understand what it feels like to live in one world. **PS**

Ivan Krastev is Chairman of the Center for Liberal Strategies and a permanent fellow at the Institute for Human Sciences. He is the author, most recently, of Is It Tomorrow Yet? Paradoxes of the Pandemic.

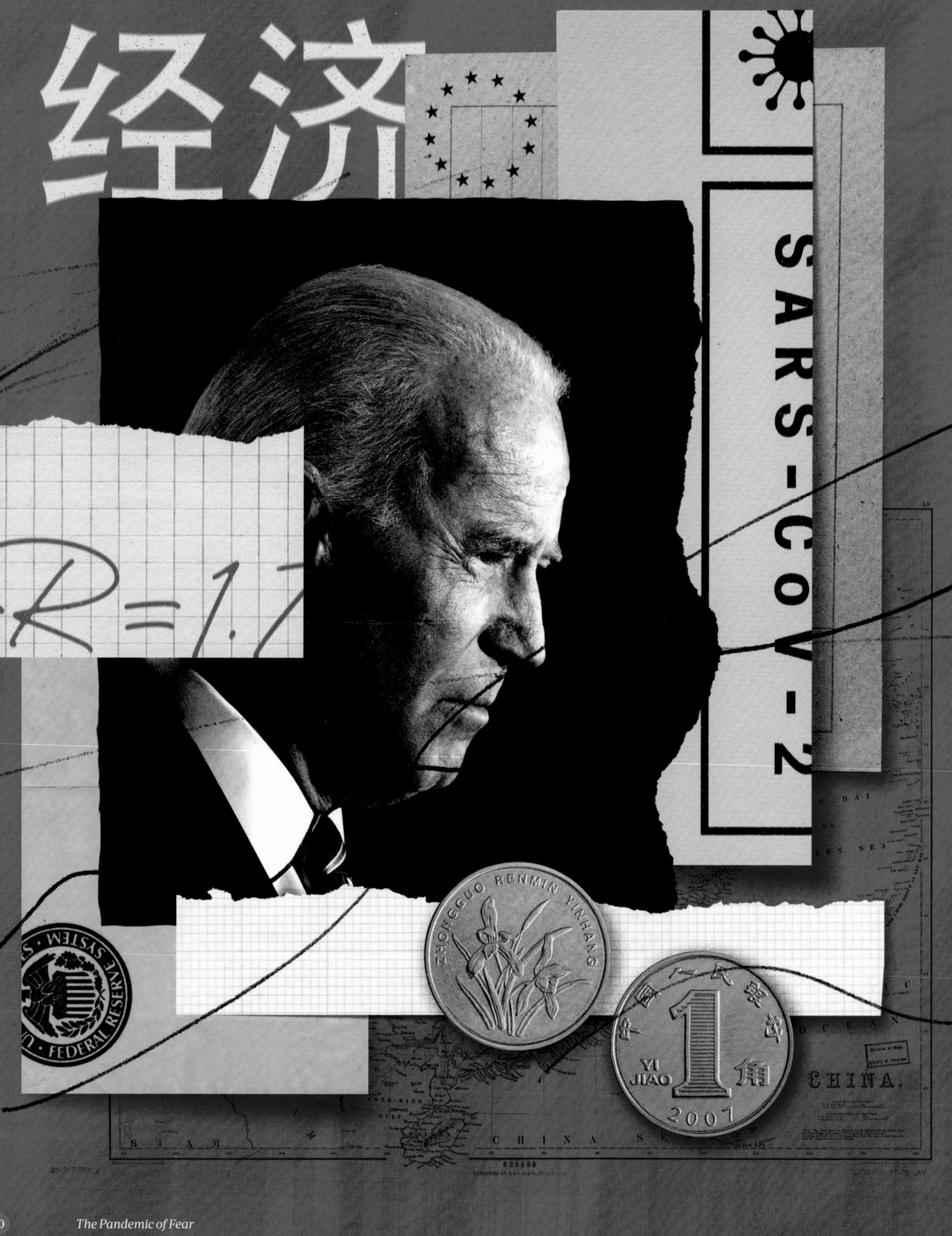

经济
SARS-CoV-2
R=1.
ZHONGGUO RENMIN YINHANG
中国人民银行
1
YI JIAO
角
2007
FEDERAL RESERVE SYSTEM
CHINA.
CHINA SEA

A Global Recovery's Leading Variables

JOSEPH E. STIGLITZ

Nobel laureate economist

As we head into a new year, this much is patently clear: COVID-19 is not just going to disappear, as outgoing US President Donald Trump repeatedly suggested it would. Although there has been a substantial economic recovery from the depths of the initial lockdowns last spring, the losses to GDP and employment around the world are enough to make this the second- or third-worst downturn of the last hundred years. And this is true even as vaccines are approved for use.

RETURNING TO NORMAL WILL TAKE time, raising the question of how much damage will be incurred in the interim. The answer will depend on the economic policies that major countries pursue in the coming months. There is already significant potential for hysteresis (long-lasting) effects. Household and firm balance sheets that have been eviscerated will be restored only gradually; firms that have gone bankrupt during the pandemic will not suddenly become "un-bankrupt" when the virus is brought under control.

In managing these effects, an ounce of prevention would be worth a pound of cure. Yet at this point, the near-term outlook remains tremendously difficult to read.

One reason is China. After the 2008 crisis, China played a central role in the global recovery, achieving annual growth of around 12% by 2010.

But this time, China's post-crisis growth is more muted, and the increase in its trade surplus implies less support for the global economy it provided in the past. More broadly, while the world's advanced economies have been able to run huge fiscal deficits to prevent significant losses to GDP, governments in developing countries and emerging markets cannot provide anywhere close to the same level of support.

Beyond the uncertainties associated with potential future waves of COVID-19 infections – like the one that descended on Europe and the United States in late 2020 – there will be two paramount questions in 2021. Will the European Union and the US enact recovery programs of the magnitude needed to restore the global economy? And will the international community come together to provide the developing world with the assistance it needs? ▶

€750bn

THE COST OF THE EU'S COVID-19 RECOVERY FUND.

The 2020 US election has not resolved these uncertainties. With the Democrats performing below expectations in many Senate and House races, the Biden administration may not have the congressional support it needs to go big on stimulus spending. Before the election, Trump – who never saw a constraint, budget or otherwise, that he did not want to violate – had been exploring the possibility of another stimulus package, only to run into resistance from Republican Senate Majority Leader Mitch McConnell. It remains to be seen whether Biden's efforts to restore bipartisan comity will succeed.

Having already cut taxes on billionaires and corporations, Republicans seem set to embrace fiscal austerity once again, in order to deny the Democrats any major achievements. To that end, Republicans will propose a "skinny" fiscal package that would do too little to help state and local governments or the unemployed. If this limited stimulus is all the federal government can muster, both the US and the world will be in for a hard time.

Europeans, for their part, have come together in historic fashion to confront the economic impact of the pandemic. And yet, the EU's €750 billion ($886 billion) recovery fund is not enough, especially now that the region has been hit hard by a second epidemic wave. Will Europe be able to come together again to pass another round of mutual assistance? If not, its prognosis – politically as well as economically – will be mixed, at best.

That leaves the broader international arena, where the US president traditionally enjoys significant

Biden's campaign promise to "build back better" can and must be more than just a slogan."

YEAR-ON-YEAR CHANGE IN WORLD OUTPUT (IN PERCENT)

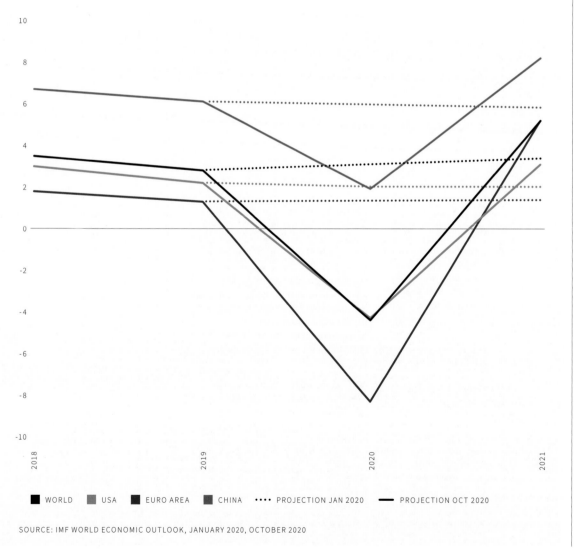

WORLD ■ USA ■ EURO AREA ■ CHINA •••• PROJECTION JAN 2020 — PROJECTION OCT 2020

SOURCE: IMF WORLD ECONOMIC OUTLOOK, JANUARY 2020, OCTOBER 2020

power. The head of the International Monetary Fund, Kristalina Georgieva, has already called for another $500 billion issuance of Special Drawing Rights, which would be enormously helpful in restarting the global economy, especially now that several rich countries have committed to donating or lending their allocations to the countries that need them most. For no apparent reason other than malice, the Trump administration opposed issuing new SDRs. The hope now is that Biden will reverse the US approach, not just on SDRs but also on international cooperation more generally.

Similarly, there is an urgent need for more leadership on debt restructuring. The COVID-19 recession has put many developing countries and emerging markets in a precarious financial position.

What began as a liquidity problem has morphed into a solvency problem: many countries simply do not have the resources to repay outstanding debts. Rarely before has the time-honored principle of force majeure – forbearance in the face of extraordinary events – been more relevant. Here, again, Biden could make a big difference by working with the leaders of creditor countries and reminding everyone that another global debt crisis would be in no one's interest.

With Biden's leadership and some cooperation from congressional Republicans and other world leaders, there is a chance to navigate our way quickly through the COVID-19 crisis. The situation demands a commitment to do "whatever it takes." If political leaders rise to the challenge, 2021 need not be the worst of times, even if it is not the best of times, either.

Biden's campaign promise to "build back better" can and must be more than just a slogan. It is fully within our power to build a post-pandemic world that is more sustainable, fair, cooperative, and competent than the one we had before the crisis. **PS**

Joseph E. Stiglitz, a Nobel laureate in economics and University Professor at Columbia University, is Chief Economist at the Roosevelt Institute and a former senior vice president and Chief Economist of the World Bank. His most recent book is People, Power, and Profits: Progressive Capitalism for an Age of Discontent.

The Quiet Financial Crisis

LOAN EXTENDED LOAN EXTENDED LOAN EXTENDED LOAN EXTENDED LOAN EXTENDED

ZOMBIE LOAN

NON-PERFORMING LOAN

$ DOLLAR-DENOMINATED CORPORATE DEBT

RISING NPLs

2020
2021
2022
2023
2024
2025

FRAGILE BALANCE SHEETS

CARMEN M. REINHART

Chief Economist at the World Bank

The term "financial crisis" has long been associated with dramas such as bank runs and asset-price crashes. Charles Kindleberger's classic books *The World in Depression, 1929-1939* and *Manias, Panics and Crashes*, and my own work with Kenneth Rogoff, *This Time Is Different*, document scores of these episodes. In recent years, the term "Lehman moment" has stood out as a marker of the 2007-09 global financial crisis and even inspired a Broadway show.

BUT SOME FINANCIAL CRISES DO NOT involve the drama of Lehman moments. Asset quality can deteriorate significantly as economic downturns persist, especially when firms and households are highly leveraged. Moreover, years of bank lending to unproductive private firms or state-owned enterprises (the latter is not uncommon in some developing countries) take a cumulative toll on balance sheets.

Although these crises may not always include panics and runs, they still impose multiple costs. Bank restructuring and recapitalization to restore solvency can be expensive for governments and taxpayers, and new lending can remain depressed, slowing economic activity. The credit crunch also has distributional effects, because it hits small and medium-size businesses and lower-income households more acutely.

To be sure, the COVID-19 pandemic continues to deliver many moments of unwanted drama, including soaring infection rates, widespread lockdowns, record-shattering declines in output, and spiking poverty. But, in addition to these trends, a quieter crisis is gaining momentum in the financial sector. Even without a Lehman moment, it could jeopardize prospects for economic recovery for years to come.

Specifically, financial institutions around the world will continue to face a marked rise in non-performing loans (NPLs) for some time. The COVID-19 crisis is also regressive, disproportionately hitting low-income households and smaller firms that have fewer assets to buffer them against insolvency.

Since the onset of the pandemic, governments have relied on expansionary monetary and fiscal policies to offset the steep declines in economic activity associated with broad-based shutdowns and social-distancing measures. Wealthier countries have had a decided advantage in their ability to respond, although a surge in lending by multilateral institutions has also helped to finance emerging and developing economies' response to the health emergency.

Unlike in the 2007-09 crisis (or most previous crises, for that matter), banks have supported macroeconomic stimulus with a ▶

The COVID-19 pandemic continues to deliver many moments of unwanted drama ...."

variety of temporary loan moratoria, as the International Monetary Fund has documented in its Policy Tracker. These measures have provided some respite for households facing loss of employment and a decline in income, as well as for businesses struggling to survive lockdowns and general disruptions to normal activity (tourism-linked sectors stand out starkly in this regard).

Financial institutions in all regions have granted grace periods for repayment of existing loans, and many have re-contracted loans in favor of lower interest rates and generally better terms. The understandable rationale has been that, because the health crisis is temporary, so is the financial distress of firms and households. But as the pandemic has persisted, many countries have found it necessary to extend these measures until 2021.

Alongside the temporary moratoria, many countries have relaxed their banking regulations regarding bad-loan provisioning and the classification of loans as non-performing. The upshot of these changes is that the extent of NPLs may currently be understated, and

for many countries markedly so. In many cases, financial institutions may be insufficiently prepared to deal with the hit to their balance sheet. The less regulated non-bank financial sector, meanwhile, has even greater exposure to risk (compounded by weaker disclosure).

Adding to these private-sector developments, downgrades of sovereign credit ratings reached a record high in 2020 (see figure below). Although advanced economies have not been spared, the consequences for banks are more acute in emerging and developing economies where governments' credit ratings are at or near junk grade. In more extreme cases of sovereign default or restructuring – and such crises are on the rise, too – banks will also take losses on their holdings of government securities.

As I argued in March 2020, even if one or more effective vaccines promptly resolve the pandemic, the COVID-19 crisis has significantly damaged the global economy and financial institutions' balance sheets. Forbearance policies have provided a valuable stimulus tool beyond the conventional scope of

> Even if one or more effective vaccines promptly resolve the pandemic, the COVID-19 crisis has significantly damaged the global economy and financial institutions' balance sheets."

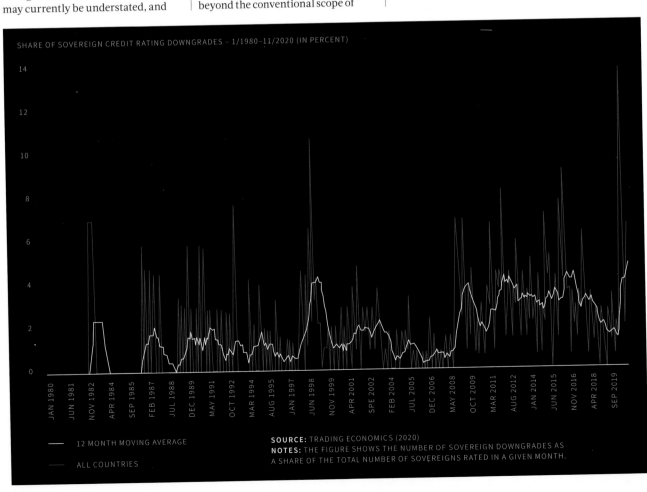

SHARE OF SOVEREIGN CREDIT RATING DOWNGRADES – 1/1980–11/2020 (IN PERCENT)

—— 12 MONTH MOVING AVERAGE

—— ALL COUNTRIES

SOURCE: TRADING ECONOMICS (2020)
NOTES: THE FIGURE SHOWS THE NUMBER OF SOVEREIGN DOWNGRADES AS A SHARE OF THE TOTAL NUMBER OF SOVEREIGNS RATED IN A GIVEN MONTH.

▲ CARMEN M. REINHART.

▲ TOP: EMPTY OFFICE TOWERS IN THE CITY OF LONDON DURING THE SECOND NATIONAL LOCKDOWN.

fiscal and monetary policy. But grace periods will come to an end in 2021.

As the US Federal Reserve's November 2020 Financial Stability Report highlights, policy fatigue or political constraints suggest that forthcoming US fiscal and monetary stimulus will not match the scale reached in early 2020. Many emerging markets and developing countries are already at or near their monetary-policy limits as well. As 2021 unfolds, therefore, it will become clearer whether countless firms and households are facing insolvency rather than illiquidity.

Firms' high leverage on the eve of the pandemic will amplify the financial sector's balance-sheet problems. Corporations in the world's two largest economies, the United States and China, are highly indebted and include many high-risk borrowers. The European Central Bank has repeatedly voiced concerns about the rising share of NPLs in the eurozone, while the IMF has frequently warned about the marked increase in dollar-denominated corporate debt in many emerging markets. Exposure to commercial real estate and the hospitality industry is another source of concern in many parts of the world.

Balance-sheet damage takes time to repair. Previous overborrowing often results in a long period of deleveraging, as financial institutions become more cautious in their lending practices. This muddling-through stage, usually associated with a sluggish recovery, can span years. In some cases, these financial crises develop into sovereign-debt crises, as bailouts transform pre-crisis private debt into public-sector liabilities.

The first step toward dealing with financial fragility is to recognize the scope and scale of the problem, and then expediently restructure and write down bad debts. The alternative – channeling resources into zombie loans – is a recipe for delayed recovery. Given the pandemic's already huge economic and human costs, avoiding that scenario must be a top priority for policymakers everywhere. **PS**

Carmen M. Reinhart is Chief Economist of the World Bank.

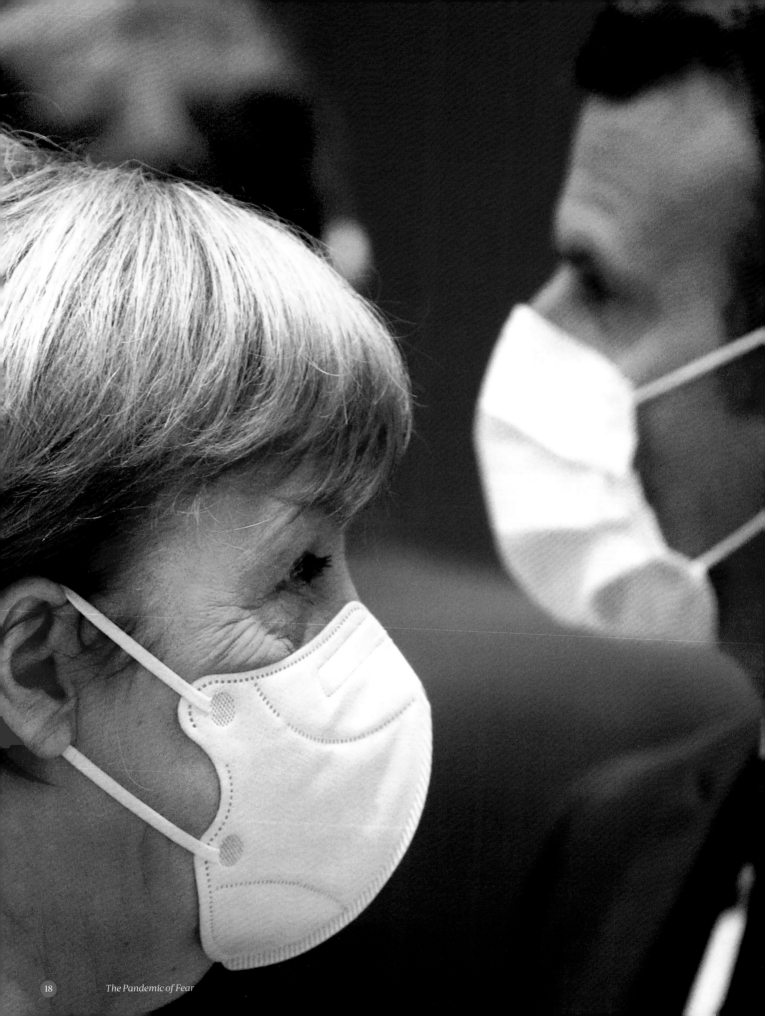

The Pandemic of Fear

pulling

Europe's Watershed Year

JOSEP BORRELL

*EU High Representative for
Foreign Affairs and Security Policy*

In 2020, people around the world experienced life in slow motion, even as political developments accelerated. For the European Union, navigating the COVID-19 crisis has been challenging; yet, despite much naysaying, Europeans not only stuck together, but *grew* together, forging a more cohesive bloc. In 2021, global cooperation ought to make a strong comeback, and the EU should continue to pursue "strategic autonomy" so that it can safeguard its citizens and interests in the years and decades ahead. ▶

together

IT IS A TRUISM THAT 2020 MARKED a watershed. In fact, the world has been undergoing several tectonic shifts for years now, including but not limited to growing public distrust, polarization and identity politics, tepid economic growth, rising debts, and deepening inequality. We have witnessed the weaponization of interdependence. Trade, technology, investment, tourism, and other former venues of deepening cooperation have become instruments of power and domains of intense competition.

This was the big picture that we in the EU leadership saw when we took office in December 2019, just before conditions became even more challenging. For Europeans, it looked as though everything we held dear was being contested, be it multilateral cooperation; solidarity between countries, generations, and individuals; or even basic respect for facts and science. In addition to several crises brewing in the EU's neighborhood and the escalation of Sino-American tensions, we were hit suddenly by COVID-19, which has compounded all the other longer-term challenges Europe faces.

The Pandemic Stress Test

There is no denying that the EU struggled during the early days of the pandemic. We were ill-prepared, and many member states were initially inclined to let everyone fend for themselves. But genuine acts of solidarity soon followed, with many countries taking patients from, and sending emergency equipment to, those most in need. Then the EU-level measures kicked in. The European Central Bank provided massive liquidity, and the European Commission authorized member states to incur large deficits to support their economies.

The discussion quickly turned to how the EU could provide fiscal support to the hardest-hit countries, and these debates culminated in a historic "recovery fund." An unprecedented €1.8 trillion ($2.1 trillion) was allocated for a new "Next Generation EU" instrument and the bloc's next seven-year budget. Moreover, two longstanding economic-policy shibboleths were shattered. For the first time, EU leaders agreed to issue large-scale common debt and allow for fiscal transfers, provided that spending is aligned with the twin

▲ EU HIGH REPRESENTATIVE FOR FOREIGN AFFAIRS AND SECURITY POLICY JOSEP BORRELL.

▲ TOP: EUROPEAN COMMISSION PRESIDENT URSULA VON DER LEYEN.

€1.8tr

AMOUNT ALLOCATED FOR A NEW "NEXT GENERATION EU" FUND AND THE BLOC'S NEXT SEVEN-YEAR BUDGET.

priorities of funding a green transition and securing Europe's digital future.

On the international front, the EU's position has been clear: a "pandemic world" needs multilateral solutions. We have lived by this motto even when others were going it alone. Our May 2020 (virtual) pledging conference to raise funds for vaccine research was a perfect demonstration of the EU's unique strengths. While the United States and China were proverbially at each other's throats, Europe stepped up to lead on this critical issue. Moreover, we did so in a quintessentially European way (call it "Multilateralism 2.0"), working with not only governments, but also foundations and the private sector.

Since the summer, Europe has suffered a second wave of infections and struggled with renewed lockdowns. Although we have far more knowledge about COVID-19 and how to treat it, "pandemic fatigue" is widespread. Worse, the initial economic rebound appears to be fading, indicating that the crisis will continue to dominate our lives for months – and perhaps years – to come. As such, we must keep mobilizing across all of the relevant domains, from public health and the economy to security and global governance.

A New Moment for Multilateralism

Revitalizing multilateralism thus will be a top priority for the EU in 2021. Obviously, we cannot achieve this alone. But we anticipate that we will have more partners in the year ahead than we did in 2020. With Joe Biden succeeding Donald Trump as president, the US is expected to rejoin to the Paris climate agreement, restore its support for the World Health Organization, return to the Iran nuclear deal, and adopt a more constructive stance within the World Trade Organization.

America's return to the global stage will serve as a much-needed shot in the arm for multilateralism. We hope that others, including China and Russia, will follow suit in reversing their selective and self-serving approach to multilateral cooperation in the UN and elsewhere.

To be sure, pleas for "rules-based cooperation" often sound less inspiring than bombastic appeals to "take back control." We must ensure that multilateralism delivers tangible results for citizens. No one will be safe until we have a reliable vaccine, so the paramount questions on vaccination are who will get what, when, and how. There is a serious risk of "vaccine nationalism" or "vaccine diplomacy," with rich and powerful countries forcing themselves to the front of the line. In early 2020, some countries used "mask diplomacy" to extract political concessions in exchange for critically needed personal protective equipment. The EU will insist on the opposite approach: vaccines must be treated as a global public good and distributed based on medical needs.

The second big multilateral priority for 2021 is climate change, another area where the EU has shown leadership. Having already set a 2050 carbon-neutrality target, we are close to an agreement on a binding commitment to reduce greenhouse-gas (GHG) emissions by 55% by 2030. Moreover, these efforts seem to have inspired others: China has signaled its intention to become carbon neutral by 2060, and Japan and South Korea have said they will do so by 2050. We now need the US, India, Russia, Brazil, and other big emitters to get on board.

Climate change is the existential challenge of our time. As with COVID-19, the warning signs are visible for all to see, and there is a solid scientific consensus about what to do. The difference, of course, is that there will never be a vaccine for climate change. So, we must bend the curve of GHG emissions as fast as possible.

European Strategic Autonomy

Finally, at the same time that we pursue multilateralism, we must build a capacity to act autonomously when necessary. As I argued a year ago, Europeans must confront the world as it is, not as we wish it to be. The EU must "learn to speak the language of power."

The pandemic has underscored the need for European strategic autonomy, a concept that originated in defense circles, but that now extends to public health and many other domains. We have learned the hard way that there are costs to depending on just a few suppliers of critical goods – especially when the supplier is a country whose value system is fundamentally at odds with our own. The solution to this problem is diversification and, when necessary, shorter supply chains.

> ❝
>
> The point is not to embrace autarky or protectionism, but to safeguard our political independence..."

This is not just about market failures in medical supplies. Strategic autonomy is about how Europe can address vulnerabilities across a wide range of areas – from critical technologies and infrastructure (such as digital networks and cloud computing) to rare earths and the raw materials needed for the green transition. We must avoid excessive dependence on external suppliers in these strategic sectors. The point is not to embrace autarky or protectionism, but to safeguard our political independence so that we remain masters of our own choices and future.

Some elements of this strategy were put in place in 2020. Europe now has a mechanism to screen foreign investments, and we have begun to address the distorting effects of foreign subsidies. We are also boosting the international role of the euro, and preparing additional measures on issues such as government procurement. As matters stand, the EU procurement market is almost totally open, while that of some others remains almost completely closed. We must either ensure reciprocity or take steps to restore balance.

Strategic autonomy also applies to cyber issues. How can Europe manage data? We must avoid the dichotomy whereby data belongs either to Big Tech platforms (with little government oversight) or to the state (including its link to the security apparatus). The EU's last major tech legislation was the General Data Protection Regulation in 2018, and much has already changed since then.

These are just some of the many challenges the EU will have to navigate in 2021. It will be rough sailing, but we will emerge stronger if we stay focused on two complementary priorities: revitalizing multilateralism and building up strategic autonomy. **PS**

Josep Borrell is EU High Representative for Foreign Affairs and Security Policy and a vice president of the European Commission.

The Big Bounce-Back?

MOHAMED A. EL-ERIAN

*President of Queens' College,
University of Cambridge*

For people around the world, arguably the greatest hope is that 2021 will be a year of beneficial transformation: rapidly recovering economies, firms eager to pivot to offense with "resized" business models, and governments talking about "building back better." The risk, as yet insufficiently appreciated, is that decision-makers will end up spending most (and too much) of the year dealing with both existing and new damage from the COVID-19 shock.

THERE ARE FOUR GOOD REASONS to be optimistic about 2021. First and foremost, scientists and pharmaceutical companies have been working furiously to develop a COVID-19 vaccine, often supported by sizeable direct and indirect government funding. There are signs that a handful of vaccines may soon be approved, thus opening the way to the herd immunity needed for economic and social interactions to return to normal.

Second, a substantial part of the private sector – supported by wide-open capital markets providing ample low-cost financing – has been busy thinking and planning for the post-pandemic world. Firms are looking to emerge from the crisis with a better balance between resilience and efficiency, as well as with the increased operational agility and open-mindedness that they were able to acquire only when forced into a highly uncertain and uneven crisis-management paradigm.

Third, the inherent difficulties of management during the pandemic have highlighted myriad leadership shortfalls in companies and local and national governments. The COVID shock has also exposed major global and regional coordination failures, and impelled a better and more widespread appreciation for low probability, high-impact "tail events." All this should serve to accelerate the much-needed adaptation of yesterday's governance structures to today's more fluid realities.

Finally, the various natural experiments forced on many countries and segments of societies during the pandemic have fostered much greater recognition of the importance of sustainability, cognitive diversity, and social responsibility. That shift may in turn allow for a much-needed change in implicit economic operating models in many areas. Instead of continuously borrowing from the future, we can and must do a lot more now to ensure greater resources for future generations so that they, too, are better off than their parents and grandparents were.

My fear is that these four possibilities are thwarted by of our inability decisively to overcome pandemic-inflicted damage. Such an outcome ▶

> The various natural experiments forced on many countries and segments of society during the pandemic have fostered much greater recognition of the importance of sustainability, cognitive diversity, and social responsibility."

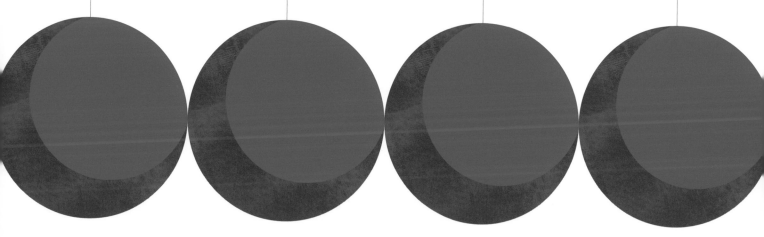

certainly would not be the first time that an imperfect journey prevents economies from reaching a promising destination.

Following the 2008 financial crisis, for example, many policymakers were so quick to celebrate victory over the real threat of a multiyear global depression that they took their eye off the ball when it came to securing robust, inclusive, and sustainable long-term growth in its aftermath. Particularly in rich countries, this lapse aggravated structural fragilities of all types – economic, financial, institutional, political, and social – and drained their bounce-back potential.

To avoid repeating this mistake in 2021 as the world emerges from the pandemic, policymakers must act early and decisively in three areas.

First, we need to ensure that we can live better with COVID-19. Despite the approval of vaccines in several countries, producing and disseminating these will take several months. Moreover, neither high adoption rates nor durable effectiveness are guaranteed. Therefore, we may not attain an appropriate level of herd immunity until the second half of 2021, and even that timetable is optimistic. Many advanced economies urgently need to repress COVID-19 infection rates while quickly building up critical testing and tracing capabilities, enhancing therapeutics, and improving communications. In particular, governments and public-health bodies need to do a lot more to reinforce the message that while being careful about COVID-19 involves hardships and sacrifices, it is the only way to protect oneself, one's family, and the community.

Second, governments must take steps now (such as infrastructure modernization, green-economy investments, labor retraining and retooling, and tax reform) to counter the mounting long-term pressures on potential growth. If they fail to act quickly, the post-pandemic world will be awash with corporate bankruptcies and prolonged unemployment. Corporate concentration will be higher, globalization will trend down, competitiveness will fall, and inequality of income, wealth, and opportunity will worsen. The global economy will be less productive and more fragmented, with less

▲ A MEDICAL WORKER AT AN
INTENSIVE CARE UNIT IN ROME.

◥ A MAN SITS IN FRONT OF A
SHUTTERED SHOP DURING A
LOCKDOWN IN NEW DELHI.

> Already, too many people are at risk of permanent economic displacement owing to pandemic-related legacies and long-incipient structural changes."

participation and access, along with a higher degree of household financial insecurity. All of this could result, on both the supply and demand side, in prolonged, hard-to-overcome structural obstacles to economic recovery.

Third, policymakers must address the decoupling of finance from the real economy, which has become so extreme that future economic well-being is in jeopardy. The last thing the global economy needs is a wave of disorderly financial deleveraging in which the unwinding of non-bank financial institutions' excessive risk-taking in the past few years undermines or even derails the economic recovery, as weak as it may be.

Failure to act rapidly on these three imperatives will significantly heighten the risk that the post-pandemic global economy becomes stuck in a paradigm of insufficient growth, excessive inequality, increasing social ruptures, and periodic bouts of financial volatility. Already, too many people are at risk of permanent economic displacement owing to pandemic-related legacies and long-incipient structural changes. A sluggish policy response will sap the energy, ingenuity, and community buy-in needed to ensure a smooth transition to new, productive, well-paying opportunities.

Engineering a big economic rebound in 2021, and maintaining strong and sustainable growth thereafter, will require much more than a COVID-19 vaccine. But with bold measures, inspirational leadership, and a bit of luck, policymakers can help to set the global economy on the right path. 18

Mohamed A. El-Erian, Chief Economic Adviser at Allianz and President of Queens' College, University of Cambridge, was Chairman of US President Barack Obama's Global Development Council. He is the author, most recently, of The Only Game in Town: Central Banks, Instability, and Avoiding the Next Collapse.

A Fragile Recovery in 2021

NOURIEL ROUBINI

Professor of Economics at NYU's Stern School of Business

By the end of 2020, financial markets – mostly in the United States – had reached new highs, owing to hopes that an imminent COVID-19 vaccine would create the conditions for a rapid V-shaped recovery. And with major central banks across the advanced economies maintaining ultra-low policy rates and unconventional monetary and credit policies, stocks and bonds have been given a further boost. ▶

BUT THESE TRENDS HAVE WIDENED the gap between Wall Street and Main Street, reflecting a K-shaped recovery in the real economy. Those with stable white-collar incomes who can work from home and draw from existing financial reserves are doing well; those who are unemployed or partly employed in precarious low-wage jobs are faring poorly. The pandemic is thus sowing the seeds for more social unrest in 2021.

In the years leading up to the COVID-19 crisis, 84% of stock-market wealth in the US was held by 10% of shareholders (and 51% by the top 1%), whereas the bottom 50% held barely any stock at all. The top 50 billionaires in the US were wealthier than the bottom 50% of the population (a cohort of about 165 million people). COVID-19 has accelerated this concentration of wealth, because what's bad for Main Street is good for Wall Street. By shedding good salaried jobs and then re-hiring workers on a freelance, part-time, or hourly basis, businesses can boost their profits and stock price; these trends will accelerate over time with the wider application of artificial intelligence and machine learning (AI/ML)

320%

GLOBAL DEBT AS A PERCENTAGE OF GDP 2019.

365%

GLOBAL DEBT AS A PERCENTAGE OF GDP 2021.

and other labor-replacing, capital-intensive, skill-biased technologies.

As for emerging markets and developing countries, COVID-19 has triggered not merely a recession, but what the World Bank calls a "pandemic depression," leaving more than 100 million people back on the verge of extreme poverty (less than $2 dollars per day).

After going into free fall in the first half of 2020, the world economy started to undergo a V-shaped recovery in the third quarter, but only because many economies were reopened too soon. By the fourth quarter, much of Europe and the United Kingdom were heading into a W-shaped double-dip recession following the resumption of draconian lockdowns. And even in the US, where there is less political appetite for new pandemic restrictions, 7.4% growth in the third quarter is likely to be followed by growth of 0.5% at best in the last quarter of 2020 and in the first quarter of 2021 – a mediocre U-shaped recovery.

Renewed risk aversion among American households has translated into reduced spending – and thus less hiring, production, and capital expenditures. And high debts in the

corporate sector and across many households imply more deleveraging, which will reduce spending, and more defaults, which will produce a credit crunch as a surge in non-performing loans swamps banks' balance sheets.

Globally, private and public debt has risen from 320% of GDP in 2019 to a staggering 365% of GDP at the end of 2020. So far, easy-money policies have prevented a wave of defaults by firms, households, financial institutions, sovereigns, and entire countries, but these measures eventually will lead to higher inflation as a result of demographic aging and negative supply shocks stemming from the Sino-American decoupling.

Whether major economies experience a W- or a U-shaped recovery, there will be lasting scars. The reduction in capital expenditures will reduce potential output for good, and workers who experience long bouts of joblessness or underemployment will be less employable in the future. These conditions will then feed into a political backlash by the new "precariat," potentially undermining trade, migration, globalization, and liberal democracy even further.

84%

AMOUNT OF STOCK MARKET WEALTH IN THE US HELD BY THE TOP **10%**

51%

AMOUNT OF STOCK MARKET WEALTH IN THE US HELD BY THE TOP **1%**

COVID-19 vaccines will not ameliorate these forms of misery, even if they can be quickly and equitably administered to the world's 7.7 billion people. But we shouldn't bet on that, given the logistical demands (including cold storage) and the rise of "vaccine nationalism" and disinformation-fueled vaccine fears among the public. Moreover, the announcements that leading vaccines are over 90% effective have been based on preliminary, incomplete data. According to scientists I have consulted, we will be lucky if the first generation of COVID-19 vaccines is even 50% effective, as is the case with the annual flu shots. Indeed, serious scientists are expressing skepticism about the claims of 90% effectiveness.

Worse, there is also a risk that in late 2021, COVID-19 cases will spike again as "vaccinated" people (who may still be contagious and not truly immune) start engaging in risky behaviors like crowded indoor gatherings without masks. In any case, if Pfizer's vaccine is supposed to be the key to our salvation, why did its CEO dump millions of dollars of stock on the same day that his company announced its breakthrough test results?

Finally, there is the great political event of 2020: Joe Biden's election to the US presidency. Unfortunately, this will not make much of a difference for the economy, because obstruction by congressional Republicans will prevent the US from implementing the kind of large-scale stimulus that the situation demands. Nor will Biden be able to spend heavily on green infrastructure, raise taxes on corporations and the wealthy, or join new trade agreements like the successor to the Trans-Pacific Partnership. Even with the US set to rejoin the Paris climate agreement and repair its alliances, the new administration will be limited in what it can accomplish.

The new cold war between the US and China will continue to escalate, potentially leading to a military clash over Taiwan or control of the South China Sea. Regardless of who is in power in Beijing or Washington, DC, the "Thucydides Trap" has been laid, setting the stage for a confrontation between the established but weakening hegemon and the new rising power. As the race to control the industries of the future intensifies, there will be even more

◤ SHIPPING CONTAINERS AT A PORT IN CHINA'S EASTERN JIANGSU PROVINCE.

decoupling of data, information, and financial flows, currencies, payment platforms, and trade in goods and services that rely on 5G, AI/ML, big data, the Internet of Things, computer chips, operating systems, and other frontier technologies.

Over time, the world will be firmly divided between two competing systems – one controlled by the US, Europe, and a few democratic emerging markets; the other controlled by China, which by then will dominate its strategic allies (Russia, Iran, and North Korea) and a wide range of dependent emerging markets and developing economies.

Between the balkanization of the global economy, the persistent threat of populist authoritarianism amid deepening inequality, the threat of AI-led technological unemployment, rising geopolitical conflicts, and increasingly frequent and severe man-made disasters driven by global climate change and zoonotic pandemics (that are caused in part by the destruction of animal ecosystems), the coming decade will be a period of fragility, instability, and possibly prolonged chaos. The year 2020 was just the start. PS

Nouriel Roubini, CEO of Roubini Macro Associates and host of the NourielToday.com broadcast, is Professor of Economics at New York University's Stern School of Business.

The Shape of China's Recovery

KEYU JIN

Professor of Economics at LSE

China's economy is on the road to recovery after the COVID-19 shock in the spring of 2020. Negative growth rates in investment, manufacturing activity, and consumption have reversed course and moved into positive territory, and some indicators, such as exports, have even beaten expectations, registering a positive growth rate of more than 10% in the third quarter of the year.

HOW AN ECONOMY RECOVERS FROM an economic shock determines how robust its recovery will be. Back in 2009, the Chinese government's CN¥4 trillion ($605 billion) stimulus plan following the global financial crisis fueled a credit boom, which inflated the shadow-banking sector and sent debt levels soaring to alarming heights.

To be sure, China's overall response salvaged the economy and maintained impressive growth rates. But as investment flooded into infrastructure projects and housing, and onto the balance sheets of large state-owned enterprises, it created even more economic distortions than there had been before the crisis. Overall productivity growth would remain diminished for the next decade.

This time around, China's recovery is again based on a large stimulus plan, coupled with measures to control the virus so that work and other economic activities can resume. But much of the spending so far has come from the public sector rather than private enterprise. Moreover, recent figures show that China's post-COVID rebound has been led by investments in infrastructure

and housing, whereas consumption growth has been sluggish and nowhere near the pre-crisis trend.

Even though people are safe going about their normal lives, the service sector is still nowhere near a true recovery. Out of an abundance of caution, people are saving more and going out less. This trend could bode ill not just for China but also for the rest of the world, since it may be an indication of what awaits other economies.

There also are at least three other reasons for concern. First, while China's export figures exceeded expectations this year, they may be more disappointing in the year ahead. In 2020, China acted as a global "supplier of last resort," keeping factories open as they were shut down elsewhere. And because part of China's current growth is led by exports of critical pandemic-related goods (like face masks) to the rest of the world, its positive trade statistics reflect not so much a recovery in global demand as a shift in production to China. This process will reverse whenever global production sites reopen and supply chains start functioning again.

A second concern is that the recovery has triggered a broader structural deterioration, following years of economic reorientation away from exports and investment and toward consumption. There has been some progress in this regard in recent years, but the balance is now shifting back toward investment and trade, as supply leads demand in the process of recovery.

China's macro-level recovery thus masks micro-level challenges. As of the third quarter of 2020, income growth had not recovered, and household disposable income was contracting. Demand for migrant workers had been hit especially hard, and showed no signs of recovery. And the labor force participation rate remained diminished since falling at the onset of the pandemic.

The third cause for concern is that financial risks are looming, and this time they are arising from the real economy. Corporate balance sheets will look substantially worse over time, especially for small and medium-size firms. Over the first half of 2020, the gap between corporate borrowing and saving rose to unprecedented heights, reaching

> China's macro-level recovery ... masks micro-level challenges."

more than CN¥10 trillion. This would take at least one to two years to resolve even under normal circumstances. If cash flows remain depressed for an extended period, risks of bad debt will rise, especially in the transportation, travel, and restaurant sectors. Such debts will pose significant threats to financial institutions as the quality of bank assets (and thus of loan portfolios) deteriorates.

Fortunately, although the government's short-term recovery measures have slowed progress on longer-term reforms, its post-pandemic spending spree is more targeted than last time, and thus unlikely to fuel another credit bubble. Among the most notable features of this package is its emphasis on investments in innovation. In the name of building "new infrastructure," the government is redirecting resources from traditional projects to data centers, artificial-intelligence applications, and electric-vehicle charging stations, increasing investment in high-tech manufacturing and services by nearly 10% over the course of the year.

This suggests that we should expect a continued commitment to opening

> The recovery may be slow, but it will follow a path that is smoother and more secure than the route taken last time."

up the economy, particularly in financial services. Chinese policymakers recognize that the domestic financial system needs to become more competitive and more closely integrated with Western institutions and corporations amid heightening geopolitical tensions.

Finally, China's recent decision to dispense with a national growth target is a welcome development. With less pressure on local governments to churn out high GDP figures, they can focus instead on boosting employment, improving livelihoods, strengthening food and energy security, and creating opportunities for small and medium-size business.

China is a decade wiser than it was when it encountered its first major economic challenge of the post-1978 era of "reform and opening up." Having matured and grown more patient, it is less impetuous about achieving short-term gains, and more invested in creating opportunities for its people over the long term. The recovery may be slow, but it will follow a path that is smoother and more secure than the route taken last time. PS

Keyu Jin, Professor of Economics at the London School of Economics, is a World Economic Forum Young Global Leader.

PS.
Subscribe Now.

Access unrivaled insights about the issues shaping your world.

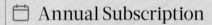 Annual Subscription

Includes access to:

- **PS On Point**, exclusive long-form commentaries, book reviews, and interviews with leading experts, delivered weekly

- **PS Say More**, weekly interviews where PS contributors expand on topics covered in their commentaries, address new issues, and share recommendations about everything from books and recordings to hobbies and social media

- **PS The Big Picture**, curated collections of commentaries on the topics driving the global conversation

- **The Year Ahead**, our annual print magazine, shipped to your door

- **PS Opinion Has It**, a hub for podcasts on the world's pressing issues

- **PS digital archive**

$100 PER YEAR

 Bring *Project Syndicate* content to your company or classroom

Group subscriptions are available at advantageous rates for companies, organizations, or academic institutions.

Please contact us to discuss a subscription plan that's right for you.

Contact us at subscriptions@project-syndicate.org for more details.

project-syndicate.org/subscribe

The Pandemic of Fear

Xi Jinping's Strategic Overreach

BRAHMA CHELLANEY

Professor of Strategic Studies at the New Delhi-based Center for Policy Research

The year 2020 will be remembered not only for the COVID-19 shock and the end of Donald Trump's presidency in the United States, but also as a moment of reckoning for China. With its international reputation battered by the pandemic, and with pushback against its territorial overreach intensifying, China's ability to pursue its geopolitical ambitions is diminishing rapidly. Nowhere is this more apparent than in its relations with India. ▶

THE SHIFT BEGAN IN MAY. AS THE brutal Himalayan winter receded, a shocked India found that Chinese forces had occupied hundreds of square kilometers of borderlands in its northernmost Ladakh region. The encroaching forces, backed by thousands of troops in the rear, had seized mountaintops and other strategic vantage points, and the People's Liberation Army (PLA) had established forward bases, blocking India's access to areas along the disputed frontier that had been under its exclusive jurisdiction.

It was a cynical attempt to exploit not only the chaos and hardship caused by China's most infamous global export, COVID-19, but also Indian Prime Minister Narendra Modi's longstanding appeasement policy. In the previous six years, Modi had met with Chinese President Xi Jinping 18 times, in the hope of

"By turning what was once a lightly patrolled frontier into a 'hot' border ... China has left India little choice but to strengthen its strategic posture significantly."

fostering friendlier relations (and weakening the China-Pakistan axis).

This hope blinded Modi to China's preparations for aggression, including combat exercises and the frenzied construction of military infrastructure along the frontier. In this sense, Modi repeated the mistake of India's first post-independence prime minister, Jawaharlal Nehru, whose dogged courtship of Mao Zedong enabled China to annex Tibet, thereby eliminating the territorial buffer between itself and India. Chinese encroachments culminated in the 1962 Himalayan border war, which began with a surprise PLA attack and ended with territorial losses for India.

That war shattered India's illusions of China as a trustworthy partner, and triggered a shift away from pacifism. With China's recent Himalayan aggression, India

▶ PROTESTS IN INDIA AGAINST THE CHINESE GOVERNMENT.

▶ INDIAN ARMY CONVOY CARRYING REINFORCEMENTS AND SUPPLIES TO THE HIMALAYAN BORDER REGION.

seems to be re-learning the same lesson. Already, India has matched Chinese troop deployments along the frontier and occupied strategic positions in the area.

The heightened tensions have triggered a series of clashes, the worst of which left 20 Indian soldiers and an undisclosed number of PLA troops dead in mid-June. By turning what was once a lightly patrolled frontier into a "hot" border and raising the specter of further military surprises – all while deepening its strategic ties with Pakistan – China has left India little choice but to strengthen its strategic posture significantly.

In fact, a major Indian military buildup is in the cards. This will include vastly increased frontier patrols and additional mountain-warfare forces. But, because Indian forces cannot guard every nook and cranny of one of the world's most inhospitable and treacherous borders, deterrence will also be essential.

That is why India has been testing a series of leading-edge missile systems, including a hypersonic cruise missile, a hybrid missile-torpedo (which can be deployed against submarines and aircraft carriers), and an anti-radiation missile (designed to seek and destroy enemy radar-equipped air defense systems). This portends substantial Indian investment in military modernization.

India's military buildup will also include significant expansion of its naval capacity. This will enable India to adopt a much stronger maritime posture, which includes opening a front in the Indian Ocean, through which much of China's trade (including most of its energy supplies) passes.

But India is not confronting China alone. In November, Australia, Japan, and the US joined India for the Malabar naval war games – the first-ever military exercise involving all four members of the so-called Quad, a loose strategic coalition of the Indo-Pacific region's four leading democracies.

Deepening cooperation among the Quad is central to America's Indo-Pacific policy, which includes a focus on the maritime realm. Given bipartisan consensus in the US on the need to counter China's expansionism, this policy is unlikely to change significantly under President-elect Joe Biden's administration.

A US-India strategic alliance has long been China's security nightmare. Yet, by repaying Modi's peace overtures with stealthy land grabs, Xi has made such an alliance more likely. It was in response to China's aggression that in October, India finally concluded the last of four "foundational" agreements that the US reaches with its allies. The terms of the agreement had been under negotiation for more than a decade.

Beyond working with likeminded states, diplomatically and militarily, India is attempting to counter China by exposing its neocolonial activities, such as the Belt and Road Initiative. And it will likely seek to foil Xi's plan to capture the 442-year-old institution of the Dalai Lama and cement China's hold over Tibet. With the current Dalai Lama having made clear that his "reincarnation will appear in a free country," India should tacitly help Tibetan exiles find his successor in its Tibetan-Buddhist Himalayan regions, which produced a Dalai Lama in the late seventeenth century.

Yet another likely dimension of India's new China strategy will be to pursue a managed and selective economic decoupling. China's trade balance with India represents its third-largest bilateral surplus (after the US and the European Union). Now that India recognizes the folly of relying on China for critical supplies, this is bound to change.

Since the People's Republic was founded in 1949, it has more than doubled its territory by annexing ethnic-minority homelands and seizing other countries' lands. Against this background, its recent encroachments on India's territory in the Himalayas could pose a significant threat to Indo-Pacific stability. Fortunately, regional powers – beginning with India – are pushing back. With this regional resistance increasingly supported by the US and other Western powers, Xi will most likely live to regret the decisions he made in 2020. ⬛

Brahma Chellaney, Professor of Strategic Studies at the New Delhi-based Center for Policy Research and Fellow at the Robert Bosch Academy in Berlin, is the author of nine books, including Asian Juggernaut, Water: Asia's New Battleground, *and* Water, Peace, and War: Confronting the Global Water Crisis.

The Pandemic of Fear

China's Fateful Year

MINXIN PEI

Professor of Government at Claremont McKenna College

When historians look back at 2020, many may regard it as a pivotal year, like 1949 and 1979, which transformed China's relations with the West. After Mao Zedong declared the founding of the People's Republic of China on October 1, 1949, the country became part of the Soviet bloc and an avowed enemy of the US-led West. But 30 years later, when Deng Xiaoping launched his reforms and made an official visit to the United States to normalize Sino-American relations, a China impoverished by Mao's calamitous rule received a warm welcome back to the international community. ▶

IN 2020, THE PENDULUM SWUNG back again toward mutual distrust and hostility. Two developments in China played a decisive role in this fundamental shift: the COVID-19 pandemic and the national-security law that the Chinese government imposed on Hong Kong.

Viral Tensions

The COVID-19 pandemic most likely began in Wuhan, China in November 2019, before quickly spreading around the world and crippling the global economy in 2020. At the crucial initial stage, the Chinese authorities responded poorly because of bureaucratic fear, a culture of censorship, and unfamiliarity with the new virus. President Xi Jinping was informed of the outbreak in early January but failed to take immediate aggressive action, causing valuable time to be lost.

> By reneging on its pledge on Hong Kong so quickly, China has destroyed its international credibility."

▼ POLICE FIRE TEAR GAS TO CLEAR PRO-DEMOCRACY PROTESTERS IN HONG KONG.

Faced with a looming disaster in late January, Xi resorted to draconian lockdowns and other restrictive measures to suppress the virus. The Chinese authorities mobilized the entire country to fight what the ruling Communist Party of China (CPC) called a "people's war" against an invisible but deadly enemy.

This formidable effort saved the day for the CPC and enabled Xi to turn a calamity to his advantage – especially given US President Donald Trump's staggeringly incompetent response to the pandemic. As a result of its successful suppression of the virus, China was the only major economy to grow in 2020.

But despite the short-term political gains for Xi and the CPC, COVID-19 may have fundamentally turned the West away from China on economic and ideological grounds.

The massive pandemic-induced economic disruptions forced the West to recognize that it had grown too dependent on China as a manufacturing center and a vital supplier of personal protective equipment (PPE). (In 2018, nearly half of all PPE imports to the US and the European Union came from China.) Although pandemic-related economic uncertainty and the costs of relocating supply chains will likely delay the mass exodus of Western manufacturing facilities from China, the country's trade and investment ties with the West will weaken significantly. The only unknowns are the extent of the reduction, and how long it will take.

At the ideological level, Western democracies were infuriated by China's official response to the outbreak, particularly its muzzling of doctors who first sounded the alarm, the blatant dishonesty of local authorities in Wuhan and Hubei province, and China's aggressive "wolf warrior" diplomacy aimed at whitewashing the CPC's culpability. An October 2020 survey by the Pew Research Center showed that nearly three-quarters of respondents in 14 rich democracies in North America, Europe, and Asia viewed China unfavorably. In the next few years, these countries will likely overhaul their China policy by working to curtail their economic ties with the People's Republic while confronting it more vigorously on human rights and security.

The Fall of Hong Kong

Any lingering doubts about the neo-Stalinist nature of Xi's regime were dispelled in late May 2020, when the Chinese government moved to impose a repressive national-security law on the former British colony of Hong Kong. The city of about 7.5 million people had been in revolt since March 2019, when its CPC-appointed chief executive, Carrie Lam, tried to ram through a controversial law that would have allowed the extradition of criminal suspects to mainland China.

The anti-extradition protests nearly brought Hong Kong's government to its knees. On the surface, they appeared to be the inevitable – albeit more spectacular and heroic – sequel to the mostly student-led 2014 "Umbrella Movement," which had unsuccessfully demanded universal

consequential. To be sure, Sino-American ties began to deteriorate in mid-2018, as a result of Trump's trade war. But in January 2020, Trump and Chinese Vice Premier Liu He signed a "phase one" trade deal temporarily halting the hostilities (although most US tariffs on Chinese goods remained in place). There were no indications then that Trump intended to harm his own re-election chances in November with a new round of economically disruptive measures targeting China.

The bilateral feud escalated to a full-fledged cold war only in the spring of 2020, when Trump's calculations changed dramatically as his mishandling of the pandemic darkened his re-election prospects. He pivoted cynically and furiously to blaming China and gave the hawks in his administration carte blanche to punish it accordingly. Xi's imposition of the national-security law in Hong Kong not only played into their hands, but also gave them much-needed ammunition to convince wavering US allies that they must join forces to confront an aggressive and untrustworthy neo-totalitarian empire.

As 2020 drew to a close, China's relations with the US were teetering on the brink of total collapse. And, given that suspicion of Xi's China in the US is a bipartisan phenomenon, Joe Biden's victory over Trump in November's US presidential election may not boost prospects for salvaging bilateral ties. At the very least, Biden's administration is unlikely to restore the status quo ante in the years ahead.

Once again, Chinese political decisions have reset the country's ties with the West. But whereas Deng's reform and opening in 1979 heralded the start of a cooperative and fruitful relationship, Xi's policies in 2020 are far more likely to lead to decades of hostile confrontation. **PS**

Xi eventually decided on a national-security law that would impose harsh penalties – including life imprisonment – for broadly and vaguely defined "activities endangering state security." Article 23 of Hong Kong's mini-constitution, known as the Basic Law, stipulates that only the city's semi-democratically elected Legislative Council can pass a national-security law. But Xi bypassed this body and instead ordered China's rubber-stamp National People's Congress to draft and approve the legislation within five weeks. The law went into effect on July 1, 2020, putting the final nail into the coffin of the "one country, two systems" governance model, under which China had pledged to respect Hong Kong's separate legal system, independent judiciary, and civil liberties until 2047.

Xi's drastic step may have temporarily stifled dissent in Hong Kong and brought him some short-term respite, but it has irreparably damaged China's relations with the West. By reneging on its pledge on Hong Kong so quickly, China has destroyed its international credibility. The West simply can no longer trust the Chinese regime, and the consequences of this will be severe and lasting.

A New Cold War?

The impact of COVID-19 and the crackdown in Hong Kong on China's relations with the US has been especially profound and

suffrage and direct election of the city's chief executive. But the CPC regarded the 2019 demonstrations as more menacing because of their unprecedented size, with one protest that June attracting nearly two million people. Giving in to the protesters' demands, including by fulfilling the CPC's pledge of allowing free elections, would be viewed as a capitulation. Mindful of the need to protect his strongman image and ward off potential accusations of indecisiveness, Xi could not afford to allow the Hong Kong revolt to continue.

▲ A MEDICAL WORKER INSIDE AN ISOLATION WARD AT THE RED CROSS HOSPITAL IN WUHAN.

▲ TOP: XI JINPING IS APPLAUDED BY DELEGATES AT THE OPENING OF THE NATIONAL PEOPLE'S CONGRESS.

Minxin Pei is *Professor of Government at Claremont McKenna College and a non-resident senior fellow at the German Marshall Fund of the United States.*

Has COVID-19 Killed Asia's Growth Miracle?

HOE EE KHOR

Chief Economist at the ASEAN+3
Macroeconomic Research Office

For decades, most Southeast Asian economies climbed the income ladder by pursuing a growth strategy based on ramping up investment in export-oriented manufacturing and services, relentlessly upskilling their domestic workforces, and leveraging technological advances.

TODAY, THE ASEAN+3 COUNTRIES – THE TEN MEMBER STATES of the Association of Southeast Asian Nations plus China, Japan, and South Korea – can be proud of their accomplishments. The region's economic transformation has been breathtaking, from its rising per capita income and share of global GDP to its human capital development and rapid ascent of global business competitiveness rankings.

The region has become the "factory of the world," with highly efficient and cost-effective supply chains. Its success hinges on individual economies benefiting from cost efficiencies by specializing in the production of key components of increasingly complex products, supported by global demand resulting from trade-driven growth. And this growth strategy remains viable today, even as advanced and emerging economies alike shift to the technology-driven "new economy."

But the ASEAN+3 economies must now continue to pursue catch-up growth, deeper regional integration, and further globalization in a much-changed and far more difficult environment. The COVID-19 pandemic has brought the global economy to a standstill, disrupting supply chains and highlighting the vulnerabilities of a system of interdependent national economies – many of which are set to experience a deep recession this year.

The pandemic has shown that disruption of one critical part of a supply chain can shut down an entire industry or sector. Governments and firms have been alarmed by their high dependence on a few countries for vital supplies of food, medical equipment, and pharmaceutical products, as well as key components of goods that they manufacture and export.

As a result, national policymakers are exploring ways to localize production of essential goods and services. And countries with large domestic markets will find the argument for greater self-sufficiency especially compelling, potentially sounding the death knell for global supply chains in the post-pandemic world.

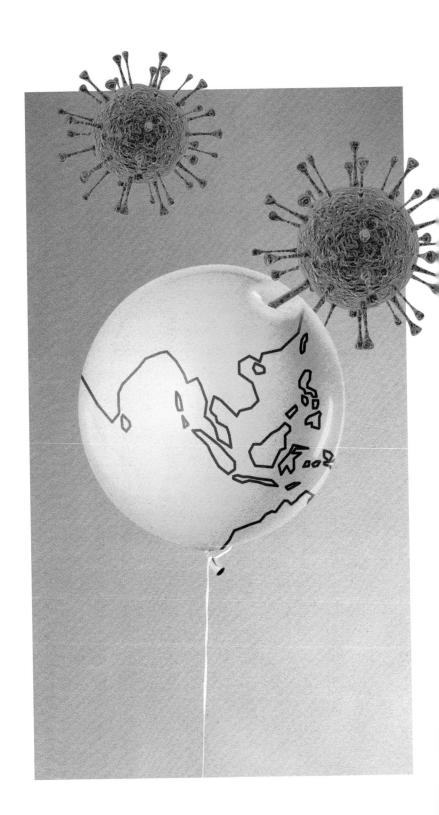

> The ASEAN+3 economies must now continue to pursue catch-up growth, deeper regional integration, and further globalization in a much-changed and far more difficult environment."

Insourcing or regionalizing supply chains would further accelerate the deglobalization trend that started after the 2008 global financial crisis, and would cause the global economy to fragment into regional blocs. In response, countries that currently rely on global supply chains would have to restructure their economies to focus more on domestic or regional demand.

The large-scale restructuring implied by such a scenario would result in suboptimal outcomes for all. Production costs would increase, and economies would ironically become more vulnerable to exogenous shocks. For example, a country or region that was hit by a less infectious but deadlier disease than COVID-19 would have greater difficulties rebuilding its productive capacity in a deglobalized world.

Inward-looking economic policies are not the answer. Reducing the vulnerabilities related to global supply chains requires more globalization, not less.

For most consumer and capital goods, apart from a few critical products such as medical supplies, economies can best minimize their dependence on a handful of other countries or suppliers by diversifying their sources of supply and building up adequate reserves. Resilience should become a guiding principle of economic policy, as illustrated by Singapore's diversification of its food supplies.

Similarly, the ASEAN+3 economies demonstrated their adaptability and resilience in the aftermath of the 2008 crisis by successfully relying on domestic and intra-regional demand to support growth, while the US and European economies were severely weakened. As a result, the contribution of external demand to the region's growth – reflected in the export share of GDP by value added – declined sharply between 2008 and 2015.

However, the trend decline in the ratio of world trade to global GDP after 2008 resulted from a rebalancing of growth, rather than a retreat from globalization, as many have implied. If anything, supply chains for most products lengthened as production locations for various components changed in response to market forces. Within the ASEAN+3 region, production of lower-cost components shifted significantly from more advanced to developing economies, benefiting consumers everywhere.

Furthermore, the globalization of supply chains for services also accelerated during the decade after 2008. Advances in digital technology lowered communication and data-transmission costs, leading to the boom in demand for information-technology services and business process outsourcing from which emerging economies such as India and the Philippines have benefited.

Likewise, more affordable air travel fueled a global tourism boom. New technology-driven solutions enabled tourism services to be reorganized into more complex but ultimately more cost-effective supply chains catering to travelers' individual needs.

It was no fluke that the ASEAN+3 region emerged unscathed from the 2008 crisis. Sound macroeconomic fundamentals, as well as sizeable fiscal and financial-sector buffers, enabled policymakers to lead the region out of the crisis quickly by adopting expansionary measures to boost domestic demand.

A similar response is needed today. Although the COVID-19 crisis has exposed the vulnerabilities of global supply chains and the economies that depend on them, pursuing a strategy of insourcing or localizing production would be devastating for the global economy.

Instead, overcoming supply-chain weaknesses requires enhancing globalization and economic integration, diversifying sources of supply to build resilience, and reforming and strengthening multilateral institutions and multinational forums. These measures will help to ensure that when the next global shock occurs, governments will be equipped to cooperate effectively and resist the lure of protectionism. That would be the best outcome for the global economy, and ASEAN+3 in particular. **PS**

Hoe Ee Khor is Chief Economist at the ASEAN+3 Macroeconomic Research Office and a former deputy director of the International Monetary Fund's Asia and Pacific Department.

How Might COVID-19 Change the World?

JARED DIAMOND

*Professor of Geography at
the University of California,
Los Angeles*

Today, COVID-19 is devastating the world. It's in the process of infecting many (perhaps even most) of us, killing some, shutting down our normal social relations, halting most international travel, and clobbering our economies and trade. What will the world be like a few years from now, after this acute crisis has waned?

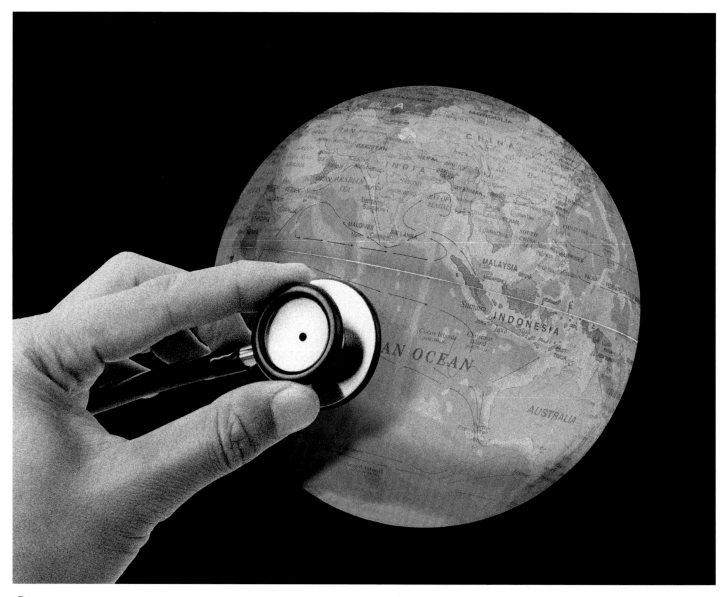

THERE'S A WIDESPREAD ASSUMPTION that vaccines will soon protect us against COVID-19. Alas, that prospect remains very uncertain. Scientists in many countries – China, the United States, Russia, Britain, and others – have been racing to develop effective COVID-19 vaccines, and the first are just starting to become available. That suggests a worst-case scenario, a best-case scenario, and everything in between.

There are already many signs of an incipient worst-case scenario. Even though some countries have developed, tested, and begun to distribute an effective vaccine, 7.7 billion doses for the world's 7.7 billion people cannot be manufactured and distributed worldwide overnight. Initially, supplies will be scarce. Who will get those first coveted doses? Common-sense proposals stipulate

> Even in the short run, no country can achieve lasting COVID-19 security for itself by eliminating the disease within its borders."

that the first doses must be reserved for medical personnel, because everybody else needs those medical personnel to administer the doses to the rest of us, and to take care of sick people. Among those of us who are not medical personnel, rich, influential people can be expected to find ways to acquire doses before poor, uninfluential people.

But those selfish considerations don't just apply to the allocation of doses within a country, there is likely to be international selfishness as well. A country that develops a vaccine will surely put its own citizens first. Such prioritizing has already happened with respect to face masks: a few months ago, when those masks were scarce and some shipments from China reached Europe, scrambles and bidding wars ensued as countries sought to secure those supplies for themselves. Worse yet, countries ▶

◢ EMERGENCY HOSPITAL BEDS IN WUHAN.

that develop a vaccine may withhold it from political or economic rivals.

On reflection, though, selfish national policies would be suicidal. Even in the short run, no country can achieve lasting COVID-19 security for itself by eliminating the disease within its borders. In today's globalized world, COVID-19 would just come back into such a country from others that had not eliminated the virus.

That has already happened to New Zealand and Vietnam, where stringent measures did stop local transmission, but returning travelers have continued to import new COVID-19 cases. This illustrates a key conclusion: no country will be safe from COVID-19 until all are. It's a global problem demanding a global solution.

I take that fact as good news. We face other global problems demanding global solutions: especially climate change, worldwide resource depletion, and the destabilizing consequences of inequality across countries in our globalized world. Just as no country can keep itself free of COVID-19 forever just by eliminating the virus within its

> Climate change, resource depletion, and inequality pose far more serious threats to our survival and quality of life than the current pandemic does."

borders, no country can protect itself against climate change just by reducing its reliance on fossil fuels and reducing its own emissions of greenhouse gases. Atmospheric carbon dioxide, like COVID-19, does not respect political borders.

But climate change, resource depletion, and inequality pose far more serious threats to our survival and quality of life than the current pandemic does. Even in the worst-case scenario, if every human on Earth is exposed to COVID-19 and 2% of us die as a result, that's "only" 154 million deaths. That leaves 7,546,000,000 people still alive: far more than enough to ensure human survival. COVID-19 is a bagatelle, compared to the dangers that climate change, resource depletion, and inequality imply for all of us.

Why, then, haven't we been galvanized to act against climate change and those other global threats, when we are being galvanized by the milder threat of COVID-19? The answer is obvious: COVID-19 catches our attention, by sickening or killing its victims quickly (within a few days or weeks) and unequivocally. In contrast,

▲ BOATS PARKED ON THE SHORES OF THE BURIGANGA RIVER DURING A GOVERNMENT-IMPOSED LOCKDOWN IN BANGLADESH.

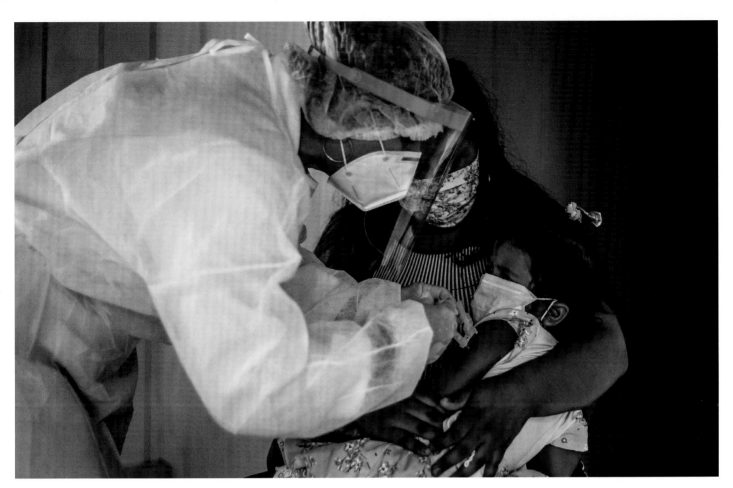

▼ A CHILD IS VACCINATED IN BRAZIL.

For the first time in world history, people around the world are being forced to acknowledge that we all face a shared threat that no country can overcome by itself."

climate change ruins us slowly and much less clearly, through indirect consequences such as reduced food production, starvation, extreme weather events, and the spread of tropical diseases into temperate zones. Hence, we have been slow to recognize climate change as a global threat requiring a global response.

That's why the COVID-19 pandemic gives me hope, even as I mourn the loss of dear friends whom it has killed. For the first time in world history, people around the world are being forced to acknowledge that we all face a shared threat that no country can overcome by itself. If the world's peoples join together, under compulsion, to defeat COVID-19, they may learn a lesson. They may become motivated to join together, under compulsion, to combat climate change, resource depletion, and inequality. In that case, COVID-19 will have brought not only tragedy but also salvation, by finally setting the world's peoples onto a sustainable course. **P&**

Jared Diamond, Professor of Geography at the University of California, Los Angeles, is the Pulitzer Prize-winning author of Guns, Germs, and Steel, Collapse, *and other international bestsellers.*

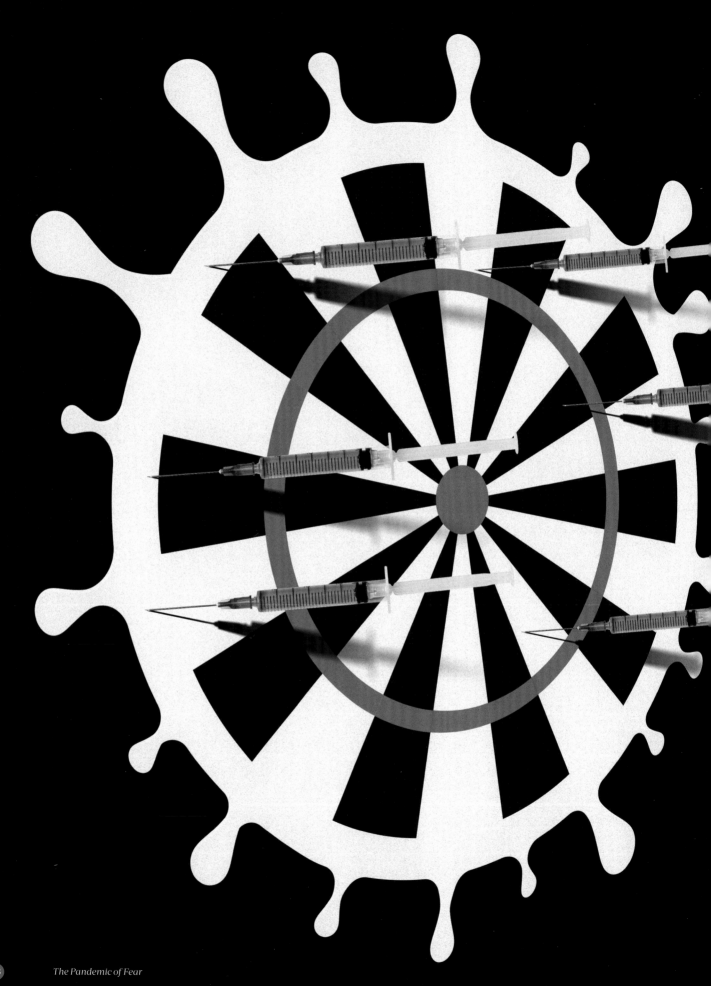

The Pandemic of Fear

There Will Be No Quick COVID Fix

WILLIAM A. HASELTINE

Chair and President of the global health think tank ACCESS Health International

COVID-19 stormed across the planet in 2020, striking first in Asia and then surging throughout Europe and the Americas in what seemed like an endless tidal wave of grief. With each passing milestone – the first 100 deaths in January, followed by the first 1,000 in February, 10,000 in March, 100,000 in April, and one million as of September – the question always has been when it will it end.

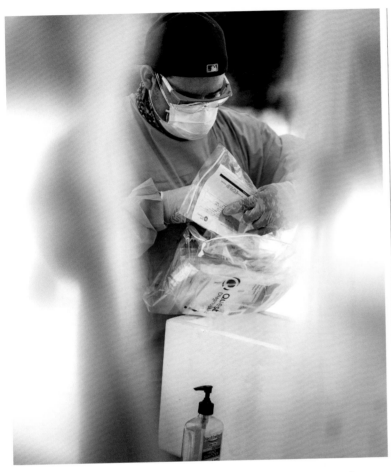

DESPITE ITS VIRULENCE, MANY SIMPLY assume that the pandemic will end sometime in 2021. But such hopes are misplaced. Controlling an epidemic involves four fundamental components: leadership, governance, social solidarity, and a medical toolkit. Most countries today have failed on the first three, all but ensuring that COVID-19 will remain with us over the next year.

Most likely, winter in the northern hemisphere will bring a sharp rise in infections and deaths. The losses will be particularly pronounced in Europe and North America, where daily infection rates were already spiking in mid-autumn. And just as the weather starts to warm in the north, South America will cool and another epidemic wave will crash over us.

As for the fourth component of epidemic control, many assume that vaccination or a lifesaving treatment is imminent. True, the pandemic has brought out the very best in science and medicine. Researchers around the world have moved faster and collaborated more closely than ever before, identifying the virus, mapping its genetic makeup, and working toward potential vaccines and treatments. But even with these incredible successes, there is still only a slim chance that we will have a vaccine or treatment that is safe, universally available, and effective enough to stop the pandemic before the end of 2021.

At the time of writing in late 2020, we are just beginning to see published results for the vaccines that gained regulatory approval in December. Based on what we know today, we can be sure that none of the vaccines under development will prevent infection or provide lifelong, lasting immunity. At best, they will limit the symptoms of those infected and minimize the number of COVID-19 cases that progress to severe illness. Moreover, the vaccines currently approved for use require multiple doses, with a delay of up to two months before the benefits kick in.

Likewise, lifesaving treatments for those with COVID-19 will not come quickly. Treatments that initially met with great fanfare – remdesivir, convalescent plasma, and dexamethasone – have since proven to have little to no effect on overall morbidity or mortality. And treatments with greater therapeutic potential, like monoclonal antibodies, are still many months away, and may ultimately prove too costly to be made widely available.

The absence of a medical quick fix will increase the need for leadership, governance, and social solidarity. Political leaders must accept full responsibility for the lives that are lost. Less than three weeks after scientists identified the virus, and after the first reported death in Wuhan, Chinese President Xi Jinping locked down 57 million Chinese citizens in Hubei province, preventing them from traveling to other regions or leaving their homes for anything other than necessities.

China showed that new infections could be halved in just two weeks through standard measures such as enforced mask-wearing, social distancing, and mandatory quarantine and isolation. By contrast, in countries like Brazil, the United Kingdom, and the United States, national political leaders dismissed the threat and dithered in marshaling the appropriate response.

Many commentators have attributed China's success to totalitarianism, but a country's system of government is not really the deciding factor. Far more important is whether political leaders are willing to trade short-term economic pain and quotidian

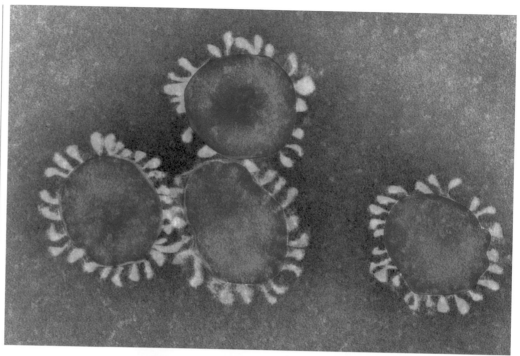

conveniences for the safety of their citizens. In New Zealand and Australia – both vibrant democracies – bold leadership and strong governance brought new infections down almost to zero, and political leaders like New Zealand Prime Minister Jacinda Ardern were rewarded accordingly at the ballot box.

The first year of dealing with COVID-19 has taught us that piecemeal measures will only feed the pandemic. National and global crises call for national and global coordinated action. The US, the UK, Brazil, and other laggards have failed on both counts. Indeed, some countries are still pursuing the foolish notion of herd immunity, despite scientific evidence suggesting that no such protection exists for this disease. There are four common (though rarely remarked upon) coronaviruses that infect up to 15% of the world's population each year, and that come back year after year, often re-infecting the same people. Assuming that SARS-CoV-2 is no exception, any country that places its hopes on a herd-immunity strategy will be endangering the rest of us year after year.

Though the Chinese government made some critical misjudgments early on, one thing it did right was to warn the rest of the world that the virus was transmissible, airborne, and controllable only through drastic and immediate measures. The countries that ignored the warning have since suffered the most, both economically and in human terms. Meanwhile, the countries that demonstrated social solidarity in controlling their outbreaks have been able to reopen their economies, though not necessarily their borders.

In the end, though, a collective response merely reflects the sum of individual actions. In too many countries, individuals fear that acceding to protective measures amounts to giving up one's personal freedoms. Yet in times of war, when the dangers are apparent, people have shown time and again

◤ MICROSCOPIC VIEW OF
THE CORONAVIRUS.

▶ MASKED PEDESTRIANS
IN TOKYO'S SHINJUKU
DISTRICT.

how much they are willing to sacrifice for their fellow citizens.

Clearly, a change in messaging is in order. We are at war with a virus. Few doubt the importance of personal liberty, but this is a time when we all need to forego certain conveniences for the sake of those around us.

Each new earthquake, tsunami, or emerging disease reminds us that nature is a dangerous force. If there was a reason why many Asian countries reacted more quickly and effectively to COVID-19, it was because they still harbored memories of SARS, H1N1, and the avian flu. Their experience in recent years shows that public-health measures that are stringently applied through strong leadership, governance, and social solidarity can quickly bring a pandemic under control and limit the death toll.

That is the biggest lesson of 2020. If it is not incorporated into national policies in 2021, the pandemic may well last not just through the next year but for many more years to come. ⌸

William A. Haseltine, a scientist, biotech entrepreneur, and infectious disease expert, is Chair and President of the global health think tank ACCESS Health International.

Apart

The Pandemic of Fear

Together

Learning to Live with COVID-19

ERIK BERGLÖF

*Chief Economist at the Asian
Infrastructure Investment Bank*

As COVID-19 infections continue to rise in much of the world, many are clinging to the hope that the arrival of vaccines will soon restore life as we knew it. That is wishful thinking. Even with effective vaccines, COVID-19 will be with us for the foreseeable future – for several years, at least. We are going to have to learn to live with it.

▲ A SANITATION WORKER IN PISA.

◀ A SOCIALLY DISTANCED HOMELESS SHELTER IN MANILA.

AN INTERNATIONAL PANEL OF scientists and social scientists, convened by the Wellcome Trust, recently constructed four pandemic scenarios. Key variables included what we may learn about the biology of SARS-CoV-2 (the novel coronavirus that causes COVID-19) – such as the pace of mutation and the extent to which an infection elicits antibodies – and how fast we develop and deploy effective vaccines, as well as antivirals and other treatments.

In the study we considered how each of these four scenarios would unfold in five general settings: high-, middle-, and low-income countries, as well as conflict zones, and vulnerable environments like refugee camps and prisons.

Not even in the most optimistic of the four scenarios – characterized by a relatively stable virus, effective vaccines, and improved antiviral therapies – will SARS-CoV-2 be eradicated in all five settings within five years, though community transmission could be eliminated within certain boundaries. And as long as one setting is experiencing a COVID-19 outbreak, all settings

> **Eradicating the virus and ending the medical emergency will require not only a vaccine that cuts transmission, but also effective treatments and rapid, accurate tests."**

are vulnerable, particularly if immunity is short-lived.

As the study shows, eradicating the virus and ending the medical emergency will require not only a vaccine that cuts transmission, but also effective treatments and rapid, accurate tests. Such a medical toolkit would have to be made available and affordable to every country, and be deployed in a manner that leveraged global experience and engaged local communities.

Yet at the moment, only one of the nine leading vaccine candidates stops the spread of the virus; the others aim merely to limit COVID-19's severity. Moreover, while treatments for moderate and severe cases have significantly improved, they remain unsatisfactory. And testing is flawed, expensive, and subject to supply-chain weaknesses.

With such an imperfect medical toolkit, non-pharmaceutical interventions (such as social distancing and mask wearing) are vital. Fortunately, most countries have recognized the critical importance of early action, imposing strict rules to protect

public health fairly rapidly. Many have also provided strong economic support, in order to protect lives and livelihoods amid lockdowns.

But short-term emergency measures like blanket lockdowns are not a sustainable solution. Few countries – especially in the emerging and developing world – can afford to lock down their economies, let alone keep recommended policies in place until an effective vaccine is widely available.

Such measures are merely supposed to slow down transmission and buy time for policymakers and health-care professionals to identify vulnerabilities and, guided by input from the social sciences, devise innovative medium-and long-term strategies suited to local conditions. Unfortunately, this time has not been used particularly wisely so far, with policymakers preferring to imitate one another's solutions, rather than apply lessons creatively in ways that account for local conditions.

Non-pharmaceutical interventions are not one-size-fits-all. Nor is the process of rolling them back. Epidemiology – complemented

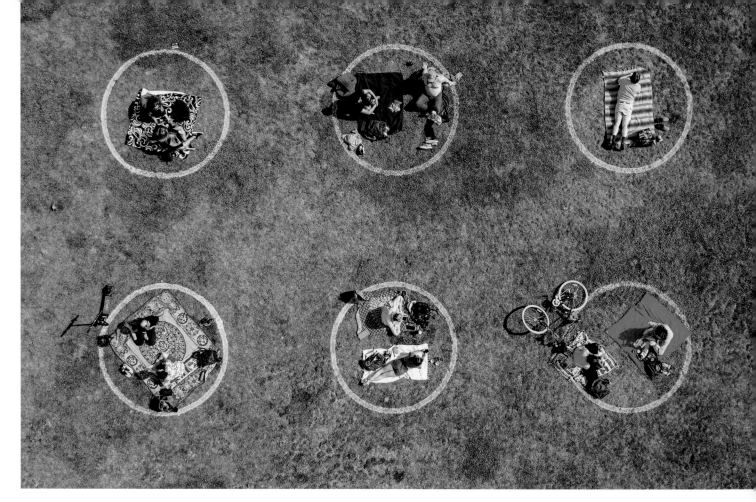

by the behavioral sciences – must guide this process.

In practice, this means that advanced economies should ease restrictions only when they have robust systems in place to monitor the evolving public-health situation and to track and trace infected individuals. And they should maintain other transmission-reducing measures, such as face mask requirements, for some time. These measures must be supported by sustained investments in public health and health system capacity.

In emerging economies, full lockdowns will be much more difficult to sustain. The pressure will be on governments to find "intelligent restrictions" based on evidence regarding effectiveness, economic cost, and distributional impact.

The political dimension of the relevant decisions – for example, about whether to open schools or allow large gatherings – must also be taken into account. Leaders must identify the trade-offs of their policy options, recognizing that they may look very different depending on the economic, social, and political context.

▲ PAINTED CIRCLES ENCOURAGING SOCIAL DISTANCING AT DOLORES PARK IN SAN FRANCISCO.

How policy choices are made and implemented matters greatly. An effective response must emphasize both individual and collective action, with people taking responsibility for themselves and their communities. Meanwhile, as countries like Norway and Finland have shown, financing temporary "circuit breakers" – as rich countries should all be able to do – can enable progress on reducing community spread.

Political leaders who think they can avoid the pain and discontent that restrictions bring often end up imposing higher costs on their populations. Likewise, those who focus on who is doing better or worse miss the point: everyone is better off if others are doing well. Competition over medical supplies and yet-to-be-produced vaccine doses is counter-productive.

So, while individual countries must adapt solutions to local conditions, the COVID-19 response must ultimately be global. Resources, including vaccines, must be channeled toward the most vulnerable countries and population groups. They must also continue to be allocated to other

public-health imperatives, such as the fight against malaria.

Already, the pandemic is fueling inequality both among and within countries. Wealth has amounted to the most potent protection from COVID-19, as it facilitates social distancing and all but guarantees quality health care. But such inequalities weaken the global community's resilience. The most effective interventions are those that protect the most vulnerable.

Someday, the world may have the full toolkit it needs to eradicate the virus and will have to focus on building the infrastructure and implementing the logistics capacity to deploy it. In the meantime, we should stop placing our hope in a quick return to "normal," and start developing comprehensive, creative and cooperative strategies for living with COVID-19. PS

Erik Berglöf is Chief Economist at the Asian Infrastructure Investment Bank.

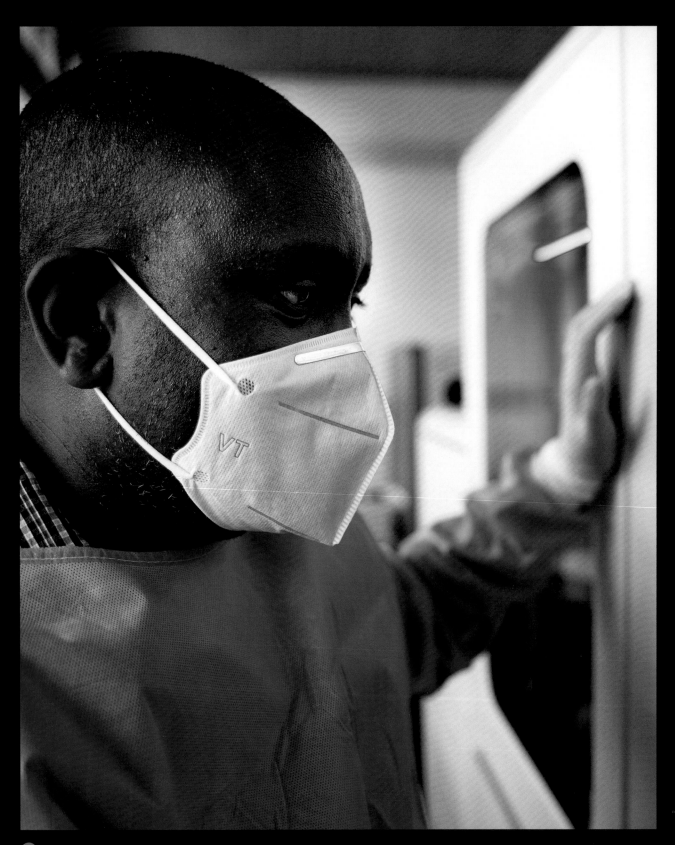

Following The Science

Lessons from Rwanda's Fight Against COVID-19

AGNES BINAGWAHO

Vice Chancellor of the University of Global Health Equity

When COVID-19 started going global in the early months of 2020, developed countries struggled to keep the virus at bay, and many began to worry about the ability of African countries to withstand the pandemic. Experts from around the world issued dire predictions, warning that the region's weak health systems would be decimated. Yet as we look back on the first year of the pandemic, it is clear that African countries have not only survived, but also offered lessons about how to manage similar crises in the future.

HERE IN RWANDA, OUR HEALTH SYSTEM had to be completely rebuilt after the 1994 genocide against the Tutsi, when one million people were murdered. Just 26 years later, the country is widely seen as a world leader in responding to the pandemic. Projections for January 1, 2021, have the COVID-19 death toll in the United States surpassing 330,000 (out of a population of around 330 million), while Rwanda's stands at just 62 (out of a population of 12.3 million).

Rwanda's success in fighting COVID-19 should lead us to rethink many assumptions about what it takes to build a strong health system. For example, Rwanda does not have an abundance of ventilators or intensive-care-unit beds, but it does have a system built on equity, trust, community participation, and patient centrism. By making evidence-based decisions, learning from the lessons of our past, and following the example of other successful countries, Rwanda has defied expectations and shown that any country can keep its citizens safe with the right strategies and leadership.

The pandemic has reinforced an idea that we teach at the University of Global Health Equity (UGHE): that an equity-based approach to health care is the best way to ensure public health more broadly. When the Rwandan national government instituted a countrywide lockdown in mid-March, it coordinated with village leaders to distribute essential foodstuffs to tens of thousands of households in need. Because those who could not work did not face the prospect of hunger, they were able to abide by the lockdown, thus keeping themselves, their loved ones, and the rest of us safe from the virus.

The government also took steps to ensure that the most vulnerable populations were tested, quarantined, and treated free of charge. And those who tested positive could rely on public support, including food and lodging.

Rwanda's health system follows a decentralized model that emphasizes prevention and care at the community level, thus ensuring geographic equity and access. Each village has a team of elected Community Health Workers who understand the specific needs of their constituencies. Since the pandemic emerged, the country's 60,000 CHWs have assisted the Rwanda Biomedical Centre, the institution leading the nationwide response, in educating citizens on prevention measures, identifying vulnerable populations in need of support, conducting contact tracing, and following up on discharged patients who have received two negative test results.

This decentralized yet integrated approach has helped Rwanda achieve the highest level of public trust of any health system in the world. Nearly all Rwandans are confident that vaccines guaranteed by UNICEF and the World Health Organization are safe and effective. As a result, since 2011, the country has nearly eliminated the risk of cervical cancer among Rwandans aged 12 to 23 by administering the HPV vaccine to girls.

Meanwhile, some Western countries have struggled to get their citizens to abide by public-health guidelines as basic as wearing a face mask in public, owing to a widespread loss of trust in institutions and expertise. If the COVID-19 pandemic has shown anything, it is that public trust is a strong determinant of public health. A country can have the most

330,000+

PROJECTED COVID-19 DEATHS IN THE UNITED STATES AS OF JAN 1, 2021.

62

PROJECTED COVID-19 DEATHS IN RWANDA AS OF JAN 1, 2021.

AGNES BINAGWAHO.

advanced medical technologies in the world, but if its people do not have faith in their government or public-health institutions, the value of these assets will be squandered.

As climate change and human encroachments continue to disrupt natural systems, the risk of another zoonotic disease outbreak will only increase in the years and decades ahead. It is therefore critical that we learn from the mistakes and the successes of the COVID-19 crisis, in order to be better prepared for future prevention and treatment needs.

In Rwanda, we used what we learned from the 2014 and 2018 Ebola outbreaks in neighboring countries, and the steps we took to prevent the epidemic from entering our country, to guide our response to COVID-19. Hence, there was a rapid push to train CHWs and educate the public

on basic sanitation and hygiene. But since every epidemic is different, this is an ongoing process. With each new challenge comes new innovations, knowledge, and strategies to strengthen the existing system and prepare for the next outbreak.

Moreover, training and public education must be refreshed and updated with each new generation of disease detectives and global health experts. That is why we at the UGHE are training students from around the world in epidemic and pandemic preparedness and response, and in managing outbreaks equitably through a "One Health," community-based approach. By aligning education with health-sector demand, we can ensure that health professionals are providing the services their communities need, and that they are graduating with the leadership skills,

knowledge, and entrepreneurial drive to innovate and adapt.

As Rwandan and other African health leaders reflect on the lessons of the COVID crisis thus far, so, too, should their Western counterparts. The countries that have struggled to contain the virus and its economic effects should reorient their health systems to serve their communities' needs. All countries should be thinking critically not just about available resources and technologies, but also about issues of equity, access, and public trust.

The pandemic is yet to be defeated. But while many Western publics are succumbing to skepticism and doubt in themselves and their own leaders, Rwanda has protected the vast majority of its citizens from the virus and built up even more trust in its health-care model. The same principles underlying that model could help to save lives in better-resourced and wealthier countries, both today and in the future. The hope now is that all other countries will adopt a Rwandan-style approach, for we are all only as safe as our most vulnerable neighbors in the global community. ▨

Agnes Binagwaho, a former minister of health of Rwanda, is Vice Chancellor of the University of Global Health Equity and Senior Lecturer in the Department of Global Health and Social Medicine at Harvard Medical School.

The Pandemic of Fear

The Post-Truth Pandemic

TRISH GREENHALGH

Professor of Primary Care Health Sciences at the University of Oxford

On July 31, 2020, my college at the University of Oxford hosted a Zoom seminar featuring talks by several internationally renowned scientists. The session was intended primarily for internal faculty, but, owing to the pandemic-inspired practice of disseminating scientific findings as widely as possible, other researchers and interested members of the public had also been invited. When my turn came to speak, I opened my PowerPoint and was immediately assailed with abusive messages in the chat window. To quote one verbatim: "FUCKING PIECE OF SHIT FUCK YOU, YOU FUCKING SHEEP NEW WORLD ORDER PIECE OF SHIT."

THE TITLE OF MY PRESENTATION WAS, "Explaining international differences in masking policies in the COVID-19 pandemic," but I could have just as well been speaking about lockdowns, testing and tracing, shielding, or dozens of other related topics. In each case, policymakers had assured us from the outset of the pandemic that they were "following the science," and yet "the science" on those topics had yet to be firmly established. Almost every new publication was contested, sometimes by fellow scientists, and sometimes – aggressively and even violently – by members of the public.

How had I, a medical doctor and Oxford professor, attracted such a retinue of abusers with the time and energy to pursue me through the (virtual) gates of an academic seminar? Who organized these trolls, and why did they feel the need to fill my inbox with obscenities and threats?

Let's go back to the spring of 2020, when COVID-19 was sweeping the world, and research was progressing at an unprecedented pace and scale. Scientific databases quickly became clogged with preprints whose provenance and quality were hard to judge. Though a few questions about the virus were quickly resolved, many others were not. Many findings were ambiguous, incomplete, unreplicated, or irrelevant, but each had far-reaching implications for the lives and livelihoods of billions of people.

Those of us who conduct scientific research for a living used to bemoan the fact that our findings drew little notice from anyone but a few fellow academics. Memorable claims that half of all scientific papers are never read, or that it takes an average of 17 years for research results to have any real impact, may be apocryphal, but they nonetheless captured a real ▶

> Once you place a fact – however cautiously – into the public domain, it remains there."

problem. Scientists like me simply never anticipated that we would be catapulted into a mirror-image universe where lobbyists seize on our preprints for their own purposes before we have even responded to peer reviewers' criticisms.

In this *Alice in Wonderland* setting, the public response to science has been so magnified that it is impossible to control. "Facts," even when generated and published in good faith, immediately are run through an ideological meat grinder and beaten into a political mold, while scientific uncertainty becomes a weapon in the hands of elected officials and unelected interest.

Under these conditions, the normal conduct of science becomes a fraught exercise. Once you place a fact – however cautiously – into the public domain, it remains there. There are no take-backs, and the longer that definitive answers to pressing scientific questions elude us, the more that scientists' own flawed assumptions, premature conclusions, academic rivalries, political allegiances, and private lives become the story. To the trolls, we are all "at loggerheads."

The fusillade of abuse, rage, hatred, intimidation, and obscenities directed at me in the Zoom seminar came from an anonymous user who had signed in as a white male. His verbal violence was a classic example of what scholars have termed "toxic white masculinity." This category of behavior also includes aggressive and emotive guardianship of immutable (but unsubstantiated) truths; disparagement of supposedly female traits (including acknowledgement of vulnerability and uncertainty, expressing care for others, and taking common-sense precautions like wearing a mask); and describing opponents with terms like "snowflake" and "sheep."

Misinformation, lies, and twisted half-truths are nothing new. But as the philosopher Jayson Harsin has argued, the post-truth "infodemic" surrounding COVID-19 is both larger and more sinister than anything seen in previous public-health crises. To those seeking to weaponize information for their own ends, the glut of scientific preprints that has accumulated in response to the pandemic is manna from heaven.

We scientists will need to be more self-reflective, developing a heightened awareness of our own identities, values, and ethical commitments..."

▼ A QANON SUPPORTER AT A TRUMP RALLY IN PENNSYLVANIA.

The Pandemic of Fear

COVID-19 may have already changed science forever. The pandemic and its aftershocks have shaken the pillars of dispassionate inquiry by forcing us to reconsider how academic findings are reported, disseminated, and shared with the public. We cannot climb out of the rabbit hole and return to a status quo of under-attended seminars. For the foreseeable future, science will be a kind of public act, and scientific communication will be a bare-knuckle fight between good-faith actors and the trolls.

How can science survive all of this? For starters, we scientists will need to be more self-reflective, developing a heightened awareness of our own identities, values, and ethical commitments as researchers working for the public good. Embracing this role means engaging – however painfully – with the brickbats and slurs. Through close readings of the criticism and personal attacks we receive, we can make more sense of the current political climate and identify potential methods for safeguarding empirical knowledge. But to be effective, we will have to put in the epistemological work of defending

▲ ANTHONY FAUCI, DIRECTOR OF THE US NATIONAL INSTITUTE OF ALLERGY AND INFECTIOUS DISEASES.

our underlying assumptions about the nature of reality and how that reality might be known.

Scientists also must become more adept at deconstruction. To overcome attempts to distort our findings, we need to identify and then circumvent the constraints of particular discourses and linguistic conventions.

Consider the Great Barrington Declaration, a recent public letter and petition released by a group of fringe academics advocating a herd-immunity strategy for dealing with COVID-19. Their proposal – that "vulnerable" populations should be ring-fenced while the "non-vulnerable" go about their lives without restrictions – rests on misinformation, but was presented as respectable science. And while it was immediately countered by mainstream scientists, the most effective rebuttals came from ordinary users who signed the highly polished online petition with names like "Dr. Johnny Fartpants," "Professor Notaf Uckingclue," and "Mr. Banana Rama."

We should take our hats off to Dr. Fartpants. The message for the trolls

is that our gloves are off, and we understand their game. In fact, I will be using my own trolls' behavior as data in my next paper. ◗◗

Trish Greenhalgh *is Professor of Primary Care Health Sciences at the University of Oxford.*

American Capitalism's Poor Prognosis

ANGUS DEATON

Nobel laureate economist

Those who advocate taxing the rich to give to the poor often must endure wearied explanations of why such redistribution is a pointless policy. While the rich are indeed rich, there are supposedly too few of them to tax on a scale that would help the poor.

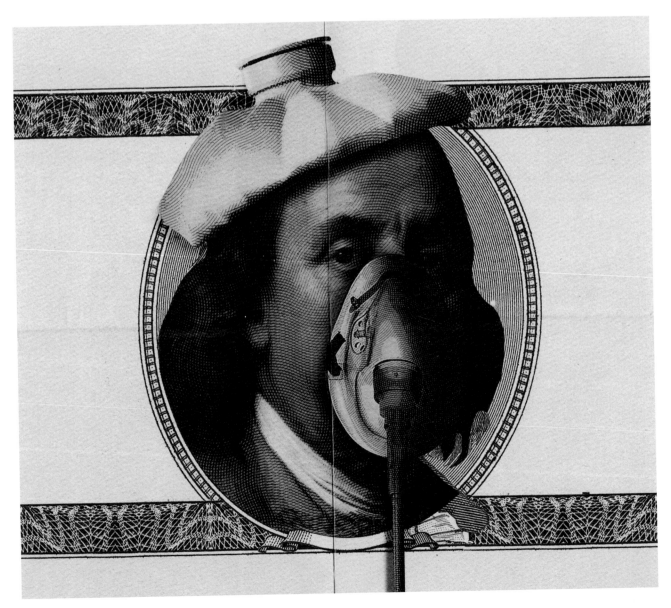

RARELY DOES ONE HEAR ABOUT THE opposite process – the *upward* redistribution whereby a few cents taken from everyone make a few individuals very rich indeed. Yet that is precisely what monopolists and rent seekers do, by overcharging consumers, underpaying taxes, and funding politicians who will protect the process of extraction from the many to benefit the few. Worse, the 2020 US election all but ensures that this "trickle-up" dynamic will continue.

The stock market's buoyancy during the COVID-19 pandemic has been the subject of much wonder. Obviously, with interest rates near zero, investors have few other places to find a positive return; and it is perfectly understandable that the market would celebrate good news like Pfizer's announcement that its vaccine is 95% effective.

The problem, of course, is that the stock market does not account for all future national income; it is concerned solely with the part that goes to profits. At any level of national income, the stock market will do better when profits rise or, by the same token, when the share accruing to labor falls. Since the 1970s, the share of wages in US national income has been shrinking. And since the onset of the pandemic, large tech firms have been doing exceptionally well, while many smaller firms have suffered or closed. Tellingly, on a day when vaccine euphoria drove up the Dow Jones Industrial Average by nearly 3%, the tech-heavy NASDAQ actually fell by 1.5%.

This perverse dynamic makes sense when one considers how the pandemic has accelerated the long-term shift in national income away from labor and toward capital.

3%

DOW JONES INDUSTRIAL AVERAGE

−1.5%

NASDAQ

▲ US STOCKS RESPOND TO THE NEWS OF AN EFFECTIVE COVID-19 VACCINE.

Not only are workers' jobs vanishing and becoming less secure, but small businesses are increasingly losing out to large businesses that employ few workers relative to their revenue. These developments in turn lift the market, which rewards those who have stock portfolios and defined-contribution pensions, while workers in retail, hospitality, and entertainment are left out in the cold.

If the Democratic Party had won a strong majority in the Senate in addition to winning the White House and holding on to the House of Representatives, there might have been a chance to reverse these trends through legislative action. The US health-care system's plundering of American households might have been checked by the introduction of a public option for health insurance, even if more radical alternatives (like "Medicare for All") remained

out of reach. It might have been possible to replace or supplement employer-based health care – which is financed by what is effectively a poll tax on workers – with a system funded through general tax revenue.

Moreover, had the Democrats performed better, it would have been possible to pursue meaningful antitrust action against the Big Tech firms. There would have been at least some chance of passing climate legislation. And the long march of anti-union laws might have been slowed or even reversed. But now, the few congressional Republicans who were willing to congratulate Biden on his victory, and even some centrist Democrats, will oppose "socialist" measures like the Green New Deal or health-care reform. ▶

> Returning to a more innovative and competitive form of capitalism requires that we reverse the demonization of the state."

Moreover, the courts will continue to advance the pro-business agenda. There has understandably been much attention lately on the issue of abortion. But it is worth remembering that the Supreme Court also heads a legal system that tends to adjudicate in favor of economic efficiency, with little or no concern for distribution.

Economists bear a good deal of responsibility for this. In the first half of the twentieth century, the failure of capitalism in the Great Depression allowed for the triumph of Keynesianism, with its role for the state. But that was soon followed by a counterrevolution that began with Friedrich von Hayek just before World War II, and culminated with Milton Friedman and his colleagues arguing – correctly enough – that the state, too, has problems. While George Stigler taught us about regulatory capture, James Buchanan showed

that politicians cannot always be expected to act in the public interest, and Ronald Coase demonstrated that externalities can be ameliorated without resorting to state action.

Less convincingly, Friedman insisted that inequality is not a problem, and argued against efficient taxation – whether through pay-as-you-go collection, the inheritance tax, or closing down tax havens. The jurist Richard Posner, meanwhile, played a key role in bringing these ideas to the judiciary. Arguing that justice requires society to maximize its total wealth, he advocated favoring producers over consumers, and the wealthy over the needy. Inequality came to be seen not only as unproblematic, but as the hallmark of a just society.

This conception of justice would be recognized as preposterous were

it not so regularly applied by US courts. After reaping the spoiled harvest of these ideas for so long, it is time to reconsider – not by rejecting all of the insights of the post-Keynesian counterrevolution, but by building on and beyond them.

Returning to a more innovative and competitive form of capitalism requires that we reverse the demonization of the state. We currently have a system in which the few prosper at the expense of the many. For two-thirds of Americans without a bachelor's degree, life expectancy is falling, not least because pharmaceutical companies have been given a license (by paying off Congress) to addict and kill people for profit. Some of the world's largest – and previously admired – corporations routinely avoid paying taxes, reneging on their obligations to the social, economic, and state institutions that nurtured them, and without which they could not exist.

President Donald Trump's departure will diminish the crony capitalism and plundering of the public purse by his family and friends. But it will not fix a broken system. American capitalism's potential to foster innovation and well-being remains unlimited, but currently its flaws are literally draining the life from many Americans. The rent seekers are, and will likely remain, far too powerful for the country's good. **PS**

Angus Deaton, *the 2015 Nobel laureate in economics, is Professor Emeritus of Economics and International Affairs at the Princeton School of Public and International Affairs and Presidential Professor of Economics at the University of Southern California. He is the co-author of* Deaths of Despair and the Future of Capitalism.

◄ POVERTY AND DEINDUSTRIALIZATION IN DETROIT.

TERESA GHILARDUCCI

Professor of Economics at
The New School for Social Research

A Post-COVID Labor Revival?

Although a few vaccines have become available, COVID-19 will continue to harm the global economy in the year ahead. And that means a difficult year for the world's workers.

THE GOOD NEWS IS THAT THE PANDEMIC has highlighted the vital role played by essential workers in sectors such as health care and logistics, especially those in precarious, low-paid jobs. In 2020, many in the developed world realized that their health and wealth depends in part on public schools staying open so that parents can work. People also saw how economies can suffer from a lack of paid sick leave, weak unions, the absence of workplace safety standards for infectious diseases, and the erosion of basic income protections when paid work is unavailable.

The bad news is that recognizing these problems does not change them. As millions of people actively seek work in 2021, many will find that employers increasingly have the upper hand, particularly in the United States. In short, American workers are about to be squeezed further, unless President-elect Joe Biden's administration does something about it.

This reflects the increase in surplus labor (ten million fewer Americans were working in October 2020 than in February), the absence of vigorous full-employment policies, and inadequate unemployment insurance, pensions, and health-care coverage. Furthermore, the pandemic-induced recession is enhancing monopoly and monopsony power – most of all in the US, but elsewhere as well – and accelerating the long-term decline in labor's share of total national income.

In recent decades, US productivity gains have increasingly gone to capital rather than labor. Between 1979 and 2018, net productivity grew by 69.6% but typical workers' pay rose just 11.6%, or only one-sixth as much. ▶

69.6%

GROWTH IN US NET PRODUCTIVITY
BETWEEN 1979 AND 2018.

11.6%

GROWTH IN TYPICAL US WORKERS'
PAY BETWEEN 1979 AND 2018.

The decoupling of pay and productivity can be seen across the OECD. In Poland, for example, productivity grew 2% more than wages per year between 1995 and 2013. That difference amounted to 1.3% in the US, 0.7% in Canada, 0.5% in Japan, and 0.2% in Germany over the same period. The weighted OECD average was 0.7%.

Princeton's Steven Strauss argues that COVID-19 is ushering in an era of increased industrial concentration. High returns to e-commerce, automation, and technology will leave fewer competitors in various markets, with corporate chain stores replacing many local small businesses. This trend will further stymie labor's ability to press for improved compensation and working conditions. The recent success of ride-hailing firms such as Uber and Lyft in securing the passage of Proposition 22 in California – allowing gig companies to continue treating their drivers as independent contractors rather than employees – may be just the start of a renewed anti-labor push.

What Workers Want

When labor's share of GDP falls, aggregate demand, investment, productivity, and economic growth all suffer. US policymakers must therefore urgently begin to reverse this decades-long trend. For starters, Congress should approve further stimulus payments for workers,

restore supplemental federal unemployment benefits, and provide more resources for public schools.

The Biden administration will still have room for maneuver even if the Senate remains under Republican control following the two run-off elections in Georgia in January 2021. It should restore labor unions' power through executive-branch measures that facilitate collective bargaining and strengthen enforcement of rules upholding workers' rights. This will help to boost labor's share of national income by increasing low- and middle-income workers' compensation. The new administration should also implement overtime pay protections and bar employers from imposing non-compete clauses on those they classify as independent contractors.

Requiring all employers to provide paid sick leave should be another of the new administration's goals. The current large gaps in provision are a public-health menace, because the risk to workers' household finances discourages them from staying home or seeking medical treatment. That is precisely why the US Centers for Disease Control and Prevention, and not the Department of Labor, keeps data on paid sick leave.

Congress can boost workers' bargaining power by increasing penalties for employers who misclassify workers and violate labor law. Likewise, the federal

government could block contractors who chronically violate labor and employment laws, offshore and outsource jobs, increase dividends, or engage in stock buybacks. And with several states having approved a $15 hourly minimum wage – most recently Florida, which US President Donald Trump won in 2016 and 2020 – a few Republican Senators might be persuaded to increase the federal minimum wage to this level.

Moreover, permanent changes to US social-insurance programs would strengthen workers' economic security. Higher pensions would help to avert the risk of tens of millions of financially fragile older workers flooding the labor market as they cash out their retirement accounts. Avoiding this scenario would, in turn, reduce the downward pressure on younger workers' pay and employment conditions. Similarly, eligibility for unemployment benefits should be dramatically broadened (not least to include gig workers) and benefit levels increased.

Employers should have easier ways to furlough rather than shed employees during sharp downturns, or to offer work-sharing arrangements, as the University of Massachusetts economist Arindrajit Dube argues. Finally, if full employment was the top policy priority, the government would become the employer of last resort. Laid-off bartenders could become disease contact tracers or teacher assistants, for example.

"Congress can boost workers' bargaining power by increasing penalties for employers who misclassify workers and violate labor law."

The Equity Imperative

Economists could have done better in the pandemic-driven recession, but their complicated models once again proved to be too facile. They sought to maximize two objectives – health and wealth – by modeling how to generate as much economic activity with as little illness as possible. But they should have included a third aim: equity.

Had policymakers in most rich countries taken equity into account, all schools and all but the least-valued and most virus-prone businesses would have remained open. Mask mandates, fines for large gatherings, adequate personal protective equipment, and jobs for the unemployed as public-health and school assistants would have been key public-health measures. Instead, school closures worsened social inequality. Many children who lack access to private schooling (or home-schooling pods), the Internet, and adult supervision will be left behind.

The US and other economies risk operating well below full employment in 2021, owing to lower spending by households, businesses, and governments. Policymakers should therefore use all levers to boost aggregate demand, sustain full employment, and redress the current power imbalance in the labor market. Four decades of pro-business tax policies, lax financial regulation, and anti-union bias mean that employers haven't had to compete hard for workers. The erosion of pensions, low or negative growth in public-sector employment, and underinvestment in education have all helped to weaken the position of workers who otherwise would take risks to change jobs or press for improved compensation.

But at least now labor and its interests are getting the attention they deserve. In contrast to the recession that followed the 2008 global financial crisis, the COVID-19 downturn has elicited strong public support for workers. Perhaps, at long last, that sentiment will translate into concrete measures that benefit labor and apply a brake on corporate welfare. To ensure a sustainable recovery from the current crisis, and to mitigate the economic fallout from the next one, policymakers everywhere must put workers first. **PS**

Teresa Ghilarducci is Professor of Economics at The New School for Social Research.

▶ AN UBER EATS COURIER.

Overcoming Trumpism

IAN BURUMA

Author

Butler, Pennsylvania, is a small steel mill town north of Pittsburgh, with a population of 13,000 people. Donald Trump is popular there. One of its citizens, Nadine Schoor, 63, expressed her feelings about the president to the *New York Times*. "I look at President Trump," she said, "and we're the family – the country's the family... And he's the parent. He's got a lot of tough love, and he doesn't care what anyone thinks to get something done that he knows is right."

▲ US PRESIDENT DONALD TRUMP THROWS A HAT TO SUPPORTERS AT A RALLY IN MICHIGAN.

POLLSTERS, DEMOCRATS, AND LIBERALS in general once again underestimated the enthusiasm and numerical strength of Trump supporters like Schoor. While Joe Biden squeaked through to victory, there are millions of people who feel – and voted – the same way: Trump is "one of us," a father and a savior.

The underestimation of such voters, and the complacent belief that a Biden landslide was almost a foregone conclusion, revealed the widening gulf between urban, educated, more or less progressive America and rural and working-class America. Like other progressive parties in the Western world, the Democratic Party once represented the interests of the working class – the white working class above all, but often workers of color, too. Republicans represented the interests of big business and the wealthier classes.

As the role of heavy industry shrank, the class allegiance of both major parties began to shift. Progressives everywhere paid increasing attention to racial, sexual, and gender equality. These are laudable and necessary goals, but this form of identity politics appeals more to highly educated urban citizens than to workers, miners, or farmers, whose identities are focused less on social justice than on religion and the right to own guns.

The Democratic Party's repudiation of these voters' views as "deplorable" or "racist" stoked resentment of urban elites, driving many in search of a new political home. When Donald Trump appeared before workers and farmers in his red baseball cap, he articulated their antipathies coarsely but effectively. A louche product of a milieu in which shady real-estate deals skirted the world of organized crime, Trump shared

some of the class resentment of people who could only dream of his wealth. Trump became their savior, and tied the Republican Party firmly to hard-right populism. Even without Trump as president, the GOP will remain his party for a long time.

The question is whether the Republicans would have gone that way anyway. Has Trump been a driver of political and social changes, or was he simply an unscrupulous opportunist who manipulated forces that were ready to be exploited? Is Trump simply the snarling face of a rotten political order stripped of its façade of "decency" and "civility"? Or did he cause a great deal of the rot?

Much has been made by Trump's critics of his "unprecedented" trampling of norms: declaring anything short of his own victory in an election to be fraudulent and illegitimate; calling journalists "enemies of the people"; threatening violence against political opponents; enriching his family and cronies; and so on.

This behavior is, indeed, a threat to the liberal underpinnings of American democracy. But it is also true that the problems – or the rot, if you prefer – that Trump exploited long preceded him: the increasingly wide gap between rich and poor, the heavy hand of corporate power, the harm to some people from globalization. Would these problems have led to an assault on America's democratic institutions and the flirtation with authoritarianism, without Trump?

Similar questions have been endlessly debated about other demagogues in history. Trump clearly is not Hitler. He is not even a dictator. But discussions about the impact of authoritarian leaders can be instructive, nonetheless. Some people, often conservatives, subscribe to the "great man" view: history is made by extraordinary leaders. Others, mostly on the left, believe that leaders are products of particular circumstances; history is moved by social, economic, and political forces and structures, not exceptional individuals.

Anti-Semitism, mass poverty, grotesque disparities between rich and poor, a sense of humiliation after defeat in a horrendous world war, a global slump, hideous inflation, and roaming bands of brutalized veterans:

▲ A TRUMP SUPPORTER YELLS AT COUNTER-PROTESTERS OUTSIDE OF THE US SUPREME COURT.

▼ FOX NEWS HOST TUCKER CARLSON.

all these conditions were present in 1920s Germany, Hitler or no Hitler. In this sense, his rise was structural, the result of circumstances.

The same might be said about more salubrious leaders. Winston Churchill would not have become "the Greatest Englishman" were it not for the unique events of May 1940. But this doesn't mean that history would have taken the same course without Churchill, or indeed Hitler. They reacted to certain conditions, to be sure, but they pushed them in a direction, or to extremes, that other leaders probably would not have done. There is no law of history that made Hitler's war, let alone the Holocaust, inevitable.

Again, Trump is no Hitler, and even less, despite his pretensions, a Churchill. But he did inflame and incite hatred and resentment that might have been channeled differently by someone else. Unless this is properly understood, the Democrats, and their progressive allies in other countries, will not be able to undo some of the damage done.

Dismissing Trump's supporters as deluded, deplorable, ignorant racists will solve nothing. Their sometimes-justified fears and resentments must be addressed. People have been shabbily treated by corporate interests that care only about enriching their stockholders. Globalization has left many behind. Urban attitudes about gender and sexuality can be alarming to people

with different notions about who they wish to be. Educated elites should not presume that they always know best what is good for other people.

The answer, for Democrats, is not to pander to the prejudices of the least educated citizens. But it will be essential for a progressive party to link itself once more to the underprivileged, and not only on the grounds of racial justice, necessary though that may be.

One way to achieve this is to focus less on matters of sexual or racial identity, and more on the economics of class. Many Trump supporters mentioned the economy as the main reason they backed the president. Democrats should offer better economic opportunities, a new New Deal. Trump promised something like that in 2016, but didn't deliver, except to the very rich. The Democrats should concentrate their efforts on delivering to the many who are not rich. Only then is there a chance to channel popular rage in ways that strengthen liberal democracy instead of destroying it. **PS**

Ian Buruma is the author, most recently, of The Churchill Complex: The Curse of Being Special, From Winston and FDR to Trump and Brexit.

The Cure for Demagogic Populism

MICHAEL LIND

Professor of Practice at the LBJ School of Public Affairs at the University of Texas

Donald Trump is the first true demagogue to have been president of the United States. But politicians who claim to be tribunes of the powerless against corrupt establishments have historically been common in America at the state and local levels. As a form of politics, demagogic populism tends to flourish when large groups of citizens feel that conventional politicians are ignoring their interests and values.

FOLLOWING THE END OF THE post-Civil War era known as Reconstruction, so-called Bourbon Democrats, the elite descendants of antebellum slave-owners and their allies, dominated Southern state governments from Virginia to Texas. The Bourbon oligarchy disenfranchised all black southerners and many poor white ones by means of the poll tax, literacy tests, and other devices designed to suppress the vote. As a result, the Republican Party was nearly eliminated from the South. The Democratic monopoly on political power served to maintain an oppressive version of the plantation economy, based on forms of labor – such as sharecropping and the convict-leasing system (renting out prisoners to employers) – that trapped white and black people alike.

Southern oligarchic politics produced its nemesis in the form of demagogic populists whose political base was among small farmers and working-class whites. Although many southern demagogues came from elite backgrounds, they distinguished themselves from the genteel ruling class with crude language and entertaining campaigns. In South Carolina, Governor Benjamin R. Tillman got his nickname, "Pitchfork Ben," when he denounced President Grover Cleveland: "I'll stick my pitchfork into his old fat ribs!" In Texas, 300-pound (136-kilogram) James Stephen Hogg made the hog the symbol of his successful campaign to become governor.

Many Southern demagogues used racism to appeal to non-elite whites who feared black competition. In Mississippi, governor and later US Senator James K. Vardaman dubbed himself "the Great White Chief" and symbolized his commitment to white supremacy by dressing in white and

riding in a wagon drawn by white oxen. But others were opportunists. At the turn of the twentieth century, Georgia's Tom Watson first welcomed black support, then championed white supremacy. Generations later, Alabama Governor George Wallace did the reverse, making his name as a segregationist before appealing late in his career to black voters from a wheelchair, having survived an assassination attempt.

In addition, many demagogic populists denounced urban merchant and banking establishments, as well as the corporations, often based in the

North, that dominated their states' economies. Other demagogues, like W. Lee "Pappy" O'Daniel of Texas, a hillbilly music radio star who went on to become governor of Texas and a US Senator, were figureheads for corporations and the wealthy.

Once they won power, southern demagogues typically abandoned their followers and joined the establishment. Sometimes they founded family dynasties in state politics. Louisiana's Huey P. Long, "the Kingfish," whose slogan was "Every Man a King," became governor and then a US Senator. Assassinated in 1935, Long was later succeeded as governor by his brother, Earl, and in the US Senate by his son, Russell.

Outside of the twentieth-century South, American demagogues could be found in northern US cities where European-American immigrant diasporas were frozen out of power by local white Anglo-Saxon Protestant (WASP) elites. Representing low-income Irish-Americans, James Michael Curley called himself "mayor of the poor." He served four terms as mayor of Boston and a single term as governor of Massachusetts, spending five months of his fourth mayoral ▶

▼ FORMER GOVERNOR OF
LOUISIANA HUEY LONG.

▶ FORMER GOVERNOR OF ALABAMA
GEORGE C. WALLACE.

term in jail for corruption before being pardoned by President Harry Truman.

During and after the civil-rights movement of the 1950s and 1960s, working-class "white ethnics" felt threatened from below by black competition for jobs and housing, and from above by the managerial and professional elite. This group provided the constituents for Philadelphia Mayor Frank Rizzo and New York City Mayor Rudy Giuliani. Trump has seemed unusual as an American president, but as a German-Scottish arriviste, it is easy to imagine him as a flamboyant mayor of New York, mobilizing other "white ethnics" from the outer boroughs against Manhattan.

But comparing Trump to fascist dictators like Hitler and Mussolini shows a profound ignorance of history. Both Hitler and Mussolini were backed by military, bureaucratic, and academic elites who despised democracy and feared communism. In contrast, America's military, bureaucratic, and academic elites, and much of its corporate and financial establishment, closed ranks against Trump. Moreover, the joking, vulgar, back-slapping style of classic

American populist demagogues like Trump, and their European equivalents such as Britain's Nigel Farage and Italy's Matteo Salvini, could not be more different from the solemn public personae of Mussolini, Hitler, and Spain's longtime dictator, Francisco Franco.

Equally implausible have been attempts to reduce Trumpian populism to "white nationalism." Despite Trump's history of bigoted remarks, his share of the white vote shrank and his support among non-white voters increased in 2020 compared to 2016. Similarly, in the United Kingdom, between a quarter and a third of black, Asian, and minority ethnic (BAME) voters supported Brexit in the 2016 referendum, discrediting attempts to portray British populism as merely white backlash politics.

As a political style, populism emerges when conventional politicians and party establishments ignore large groups of a country's population. Examples include white farmers and workers in the antebellum US South, Midwestern farmers in the late nineteenth century, Euro-American "white ethnics" in

▲ BOSTON POLITICIAN JAMES MICHAEL CURLEY.

▼ LEAVE VOTERS BEFORE THE UK'S BREXIT REFERENDUM.

"American history shows that the best way to eliminate populism is to incorporate alienated constituencies into mainstream politics..."

the twentieth-century Northeast, and working-class whites in the industrial Midwest and northern Britain in the twenty-first century.

To be sure, populist demagogues frequently promote crackpot measures to solve real problems. William Jennings Bryan, a three-time Democratic presidential nominee, pushed monetary bimetallism (back the dollar with silver, in addition to gold) as a panacea for suffering farmers. But even if their colorful champions are crooks or charlatans, desperate voters often have legitimate grievances.

Today, industrial offshoring and immigration produce losers as well as winners. The US establishment taboo against acknowledging the downsides of free trade and immigration gave Trump issues he could exploit, just as the bipartisan orthodoxy in favor of the deflationary gold standard did for Bryan in the 1890s. But Trump's wall along the US-Mexico border and his slapdash use of tariffs, like Bryan's promotion of silver coinage, have been gimmicks rather than credible policies.

American history shows that the best way to eliminate populism is to incorporate alienated constituencies into mainstream politics and address their legitimate grievances by sophisticated means. President Franklin D. Roosevelt's New Deal achieved many of the goals of Bryan's agrarian populist movement. But it did so by bringing farmers and workers into politics and policymaking in an institutionalized way, through farm organizations and labor unions. During the Great Depression, Roosevelt achieved one populist goal by abandoning the gold standard, a system that most economists today agree was economically harmful. But this and other legitimate populist grievances were addressed by New Deal reformers inside the two-party system and the national establishment, not by inflammatory outsiders.

Populists are often scoundrels, but their followers deserve to be respected and heard. Demagogic populism is a disease of representative democracy. Curing it requires democracy to be truly representative. ⓑ

Michael Lind is Professor of Practice at the Lyndon B. Johnson School of Public Affairs at the University of Texas at Austin and author of The New Class War: Saving Democracy from the Managerial Elite.

▼ DONALD TRUMP AT A CAMPAIGN RALLY IN INDIANA.

The Pandemic of Fear

America's Post-Trump Reckoning

HAROLD HONGJU KOH

*Professor of International Law
at Yale Law School*

Whether America can restore its global standing over the next four years will depend on the American people's ability to come together, as a nation, to lead the world in addressing global problems in a manner consistent with the rule of law.

DURING THE FIRST THREE YEARS OF Donald Trump's presidency, America faced mostly self-inflicted crises, but the COVID-19 disaster cast Trump's signature weaknesses in stark relief: topsy-turvy policymaking, unbridled mendacity, and conspiracy mongering. Everyone now appreciates the profound deficiencies of Trump's obsession with "deals." His transactional approach – marked by cascades of threats, tit-for-tat retaliations, abrupt reversals, and hollow photo-ops – has devastated longstanding relationships and alliances originally built on genuine bonds of mutual interest, affection, confidence, trust, cooperation, and sacrifice.

Worse, Trump's contempt for relationships was paired with an equally stunning scorn for truth, diplomacy, bureaucracy, and other essential ingredients of sound administration, at both the national and the multilateral level. His startling disregard for expertise and science has resulted in the erosion and degradation of previously independent and effective national institutions such as the US Postal Service, the

Centers for Disease Control and Prevention, the Environmental Protection Agency, the Food and Drug Administration, the FBI, and the US intelligence community.

As Trump's presidency lurched into its fourth chaotic year, his disastrous response to the COVID-19 pandemic laid bare his flawed overall approach to governing. His failure to implement a national plan to provide testing, protective equipment, ventilators, paycheck protections, contact tracing, or, looking ahead, vaccine delivery, intersected with his administration's bullheaded efforts to undermine Americans' health care through reactionary judicial appointments. And America's complete disengagement from any coordinated global effort to tackle the pandemic all but ensured that the dual public health and economic crises would spin out of control.

The result has been a harrowing decline in America's longstanding reputation for competence. By trashing the US tradition of constructive engagement with (admittedly imperfect) multilateral institutions, Trump has encouraged a destructive race to the bottom ▶

on key economic and climate issues, triggering a dangerous trend toward vaccine nationalism. Instead of standing for truth, justice, and the "American way," he and his cronies have transformed America into a sad exemplar of deception, opportunism, and beggar-thy-neighbor dissembling.

Perhaps most fundamentally, as the recent election only confirmed, Trump has shown contempt for the values and institutions underpinning the rule of law. These include free and fair elections, the peaceful transfer of power, an independent judiciary and civil service, non-political prosecutions, independent media, and protections for racial, religious, and sexual minorities.

Reliable rules of international law, particularly when internalized into national law, have long given private and public economic actors the necessary assurance that a predictable transnational legal process will protect their interests when they operate abroad. But Trump evinced little respect for the underpinnings of investor confidence: reliability, due process, regulatory stability, the protection of settled expectations, and the preservation of like-for-like outcomes.

Geopolitically, Trump has been at his most destructive when weakening US alliances, multilateral organizations, and international dispute-settlement mechanisms. Such institutions are desperately needed to facilitate solutions to global crises like pandemics, forced migration, and climate change. For decades, successive US administrations from both parties had pursued an external strategy of "Engage, Translate, and Leverage" when it came to global problems. When in doubt, US leaders would engage with allies and adversaries, translate existing legal rules to new situations, and leverage lawful responses into broader, stable strategic solutions.

But Trump has pursued the diametrically opposite philosophy: "Disengage, Black Hole, and Go it alone." When in doubt, his administration disengaged, argued that new situations presented "black holes" to which no law applies, and substituted unilateral browbeating for stabilizing long-term solutions.

Trump sought to replace the post-World War II Kantian vision of a community of democracies cooperating on the basis of shared values with a values-free Orwellian vision of great-power spheres of influence. The Orwellian vision is not only repugnant to core American values; it also offers no plausible answer to any of America's three looming national reckonings. The US faces an economic reckoning over the problem of inequality; a cultural reckoning over the question of how to accommodate diversity and inclusion at a time of growing political polarization; and a global reckoning born of the need for international cooperation in an age of virulent zero-sum nationalism.

Reclaiming the Soul of the Nation

Against this backdrop, President-elect Joe Biden's administration will have its work cut out for it. Among its most urgent priorities will be to re-enter the Paris climate accord, the World Health Organization, and some variation on the Iran nuclear deal. Biden probably will restore US participation in the United Nations Human Rights Council, UNESCO, and the Arms Trade Treaty as well. And he should lift the counterproductive punitive sanctions on International Criminal Court official, and end the US veto on judges appointed to the World Trade Organization's Appellate Body.

The logistics of rejoining each of these bodies will need to be addressed on a case-by-case basis. New treaty ratifications will be hard, of course, given the sharply divided US Senate. The two treaties that could attract bipartisan support are a five-year extension of New START (the Strategic Arms Reduction Treaty) and the UN Convention on the Law of the Sea (UNCLOS), whose ratification has been supported by top foreign-policy officials in both Democratic and Republican administrations for more than 20 years.

While Republican senators have consistently opposed UNCLOS on sovereignty grounds, their opposition has become increasingly nonsensical. By not ratifying the convention, the US has ceded dominance to the Russians in the Arctic and to China in the South China Sea. Moreover, the Biden administration should seek Senate support to ratify the Framework Convention on Tobacco Control, and to end the shameful US non-ratification of the Convention

> Given how much the world has changed these past four years, the Biden administration cannot simply restore a pre-Trump status quo."

on the Rights of the Child and the Convention on the Elimination of All Forms of Discrimination Against Women. Likewise, closing the US detention camp at Guantánamo would finally kill an albatross that has been hanging around America's neck since the George W. Bush administration.

Biden also will need to move quickly to fill the global-governance vacuums that Trump created, and which Russia and China have been eager to exploit. Russia has been acting with impunity as it attempts to murder leading opposition figures, supports autocrats like Aleksandr Lukashenko in Belarus, and launches cyber and military campaigns against Estonia, Georgia, Ukraine, and other countries. China has gone even further, seeking to supplant the US-led Bretton Woods institutions with its own institutional creations, including the Asian Infrastructure Investment Bank and the Belt and Road Initiative.

But given how much the world has changed these past four years, the Biden administration cannot simply restore a pre-Trump status quo. As it re-engages with US partners and allies, it will have to provide

assurances that arrangements made in the next four years will survive into the future. To that end, Biden may decide to re-engage aggressively through nonbinding political agreements or "executive agreements plus" (international compacts that are not expressly approved by Congress, but that arguably comport with existing legislative frameworks).

This form of engagement may seem less robust. But as I have shown elsewhere, twenty-first-century international legal engagement has increasingly expanded beyond traditional tools like treaties and international agreements. It now regularly allows for nonlegal understandings, layered cooperation, and diplomatic "law talk": international conversations about evolving global norms that memorialize a mutual understanding on paper without creating binding legal agreements. Because these soft-law tools have proven effective in legal "regime building," it is now common for international legal arrangements and institutions to be developed less through formal devices and more through repeated bilateral, plurilateral, and multilateral dialogue among international lawyers from different countries.

As these regimes take shape, stakeholders start by defining new soft norms, and then work through an iterative process to set standard practices of layered private and public cooperation, as was done with the recent Oxford Statements on International Law Protections Against Cyberoperations Targeting the Health Care Sector, Safeguarding Vaccine Research, and Election Security.

The best hope for a more bipartisan, Congress-inclusive approach to US international re-engagement would be for Biden, House Speaker Nancy Pelosi, and Senate Majority Leader Mitch McConnell to agree to an expedited joint-resolution process, similar to the one already used in trade policy. This would allow for timely up-or-down floor votes on amendable agreement packages, giving Congress more input and Biden the vital legislative support he needs for effective international lawmaking.

This daunting "to-do list" will test not only the new administration's bandwidth but also its political skills. With luck, Biden's cabinet will include savvy professionals and longtime legislators, giving a prominent role to former senator and Vice President-elect Kamala Harris. When coupled with Biden's long history of bipartisan cooperation, a competent, experienced team can forge a new political consensus (both domestically and internationally), restore America's global commitments, and confront the country's three reckonings head on.

After four years of trauma, Americans and their allies badly need a lasting course correction. It won't be easy, but neither is it impossible. Biden has more high-level legislative experience than any US president since Lyndon B. Johnson. And, as always, we will need a little help from our friends. PS

Harold Hongju Koh, *Professor of International Law and former dean of Yale Law School, served as Legal Adviser (2009–13) at the US State Department and as Assistant US Secretary of State for Democracy, Human Rights, and Labor (1998–2001). He is the author, most recently, of* The Trump Administration and International Law.

Recovering Global Leadership

SRI MULYANI INDRAWATI
Minister of Finance of Indonesia

This year, the world experienced a global crisis unlike anything seen in generations. The COVID-19 pandemic is indiscriminate and unprecedented in scale, and has exposed pervasive weaknesses in health systems, emergency preparedness, and multilateral coordination. Though the coronavirus is primarily a health issue, it remains a multidimensional crisis.

OWING TO THE SHEER COMPLEXITY OF the pandemic's fallout, policymakers at all levels have been confronted with unprecedented challenges. Governments have had to strike a balance between protecting lives and livelihoods, and maintaining fiscal space and avoiding higher debt burdens. During these extraordinary times, the trade-offs between speed, accuracy, and effectiveness in policymaking have become widely apparent.

Though most national governments have responded to the crisis in a similar overall fashion, the effectiveness of policies has varied widely across countries, reflecting differences in political leadership, institutional capacity, decision-making processes, and other factors. Robust and inclusive health-care systems, emergency preparedness, and social safety nets have all played a critical role. In the future, these systems, along with sound macroeconomic policy and available fiscal space, will allow countries to respond faster and more effectively to similar shocks.

And such shocks can be sharp and, worse, synchronous. From January to April this year, the global economy plunged from general optimism to the worst downturn since the Great Depression. The World Bank estimates that as many as 100 million people will be pushed into extreme poverty, reversing decades of progress.

Across developing countries, the burden of COVID-19 and the ensuing lockdown measures has fallen the hardest on workers and households that lack access to adequate social safety nets. Without an expansion of assistance, the near-poor and other vulnerable groups could easily fall into deeper penury. But the efficacy and pace of a government's response depends heavily on the availability and reliability of data. Countries that already have detailed, easily accessible information about potential beneficiaries can adjust their programs very quickly to target at-risk populations. For those without unified databases, however, expanding the data in the midst of a pandemic poses significant challenges.

For its part, Indonesia, like most countries, has responded to the pandemic by reinforcing its public-health infrastructure, expanding social protections, and extending support to small businesses. With a unified household database for the bottom 40% of the population already available, we have been able to expand eligibility for benefits quickly, with the goal of covering the bottom 60% of households.

Whereas small businesses and the informal sector were relatively well-cushioned from previous economic crises, these constituencies have now been among the most vulnerable to pandemic lockdown measures. Like many other countries, ▶

100m

THE WORLD BANK'S ESTIMATE OF THE NUMBER OF PEOPLE WHO COULD BE PUSHED INTO EXTREME POVERTY BY THE PANDEMIC.

Indonesia has therefore emphasized policies to support small businesses, including through subsidized interest rates, debt restructuring, and working-capital loans combined with credit guarantees.

Looking toward 2021, it is already clear that the shape and pace of a global recovery will depend on several related factors. But the most important is global leadership. The international community needs to agree on a common platform for driving a recovery that is consistent with the 2030 Sustainable Development Goals (SDGs).

Yet, whereas G20 leaders came together in the aftermath of the 2008 financial crisis to save the world economy from a deeper collapse, we are now facing an unprecedented lack of global leadership. The United States and China are locked in a conflict over trade, 5G technology, and other geopolitical issues, and multilateral systems and processes have been sidelined in the name of national sovereignty.

In the absence of global leadership, each country is left to focus on what it can do domestically to avoid the worst-case scenario of a protracted pandemic while maintaining progress toward the SDGs. For example, Indonesia's social protection programs and policies in support of small businesses include special carve-outs for women beneficiaries. This approach not only improves financial inclusion for women, but also advances other development goals, because women tend to allocate more resource to children.

Policymakers must also reckon with the pandemic's impact on how people work and interact,

But even as governments focus on domestic challenges in the near term, global cooperation ultimately will be critical to secure a sustainable and inclusive recovery."

▼ AN INDONESIAN POLICE OFFICER DISINFECTS MOTORISTS' VEHICLES IN MOJOKERTO.

The Pandemic of Fear

and with sharply higher reliance on digital technologies and Internet infrastructure. The COVID disruption thus represents an opportunity to transform the economy through more efficient, effective, and flexible working arrangements and a reduced carbon footprint. Investments in digital technology and infrastructure are both valuable in themselves and powerful catalysts for economic recovery.

Moreover, with narrowing fiscal capacity everywhere, reforms to improve the quality of public spending have become increasingly important. Transparent policy design, accurate data, and effective institutions are all crucial to ensure that all public resources are spent on what really matters for development.

But even as governments focus on domestic challenges in the near term, global cooperation ultimately will be critical to secure a sustainable and inclusive recovery. Concerted international collaboration is needed to manage the upcoming debt tsunami that the pandemic has set in motion. Many countries were already struggling with unsustainable debt burdens before

the crisis, and it will take global cooperation to avoid sweeping credit downgrades and a wave of sovereign debt crises in the months ahead.

Moreover, because the pandemic will not be defeated until the virus has been eradicated in all countries, global cooperation will be needed to ensure universal access to vaccines. Without universal vaccination, COVID-19 will further widen the gap between rich and poor, exacerbating social and political instability within and across countries.

So far, the world has managed to avoid the worst-case scenario, having heeded many of the lessons of the 2008 crisis. But we have yet to pass the pandemic test. The 2020 crisis has shown us that we need even more global cooperation in order to face this century's toughest challenges.

The global recovery is now on the line. We must reform and revive the multilateral system and resist those who would throw the baby out with the bathwater. The global economy is one boat carrying the fate of eight billion people. Its recovery is in the interest of every business, every national government, and every multilateral forum. PS

Sri Mulyani Indrawati is Minister of Finance of Indonesia.

NEW YORK TIMES BESTSELLER

Deaths of Despair and the Future of Capitalism

Anne Case & Angus Deaton

"Of the highest importance."—Martin Wolf, *Financial Times*

Paperback available March 2021

NEW YORK TIMES
BESTSELLER

WALL STREET JOURNAL
BESTSELLER

A *NEW YORK TIMES BOOK REVIEW*
EDITORS' CHOICE

SHORTLISTED FOR THE
FINANCIAL TIMES AND MCKINSEY
BUSINESS BOOK OF THE YEAR

A *NEW STATESMAN*
BOOK TO READ

A *NEW YORK TIMES*
NOTABLE BOOK OF 2020

**FROM ECONOMIST ANNE CASE AND
NOBEL PRIZE WINNER ANGUS DEATON,**
a groundbreaking account of how the flaws in
capitalism are fatal for America's working class

"Remarkable."
—John Harris, *The Guardian*

"Painfully relevant."
—Carlos Lozada, *Washington Post*

"An excellent book."
—Nicholas Kristof, *New York Times*

"[A] hard-hitting study of US capitalism."
—Andrew Robinson, *Nature*

"This book is of the highest importance."
—Martin Wolf, *Financial Times*

"[A] well-argued, important book."
—Rosamund Urwin, *Sunday Times*

AVAILABLE NOW IN HARDCOVER, EBOOK, AND AUDIO

PRINCETON UNIVERSITY PRESS

The Pandemic of Fear

Debt and Disease

MARTÍN GUZMÁN

Minister of Economy of Argentina

The COVID-19 pandemic will undoubtedly be remembered as one of the most difficult episodes in the history of modern capitalism. But it is difficult for different countries in different ways, which is reflected in the policies their governments have adopted. And nowhere are the difficulties greater than in highly indebted countries.

IN ARGENTINA, THE PANDEMIC HIT at a time when the country had no access to credit. In that context, we initiated and finalized a sovereign-debt restructuring that has – for the first time – tested the collective-action clauses (CACs) that became the new market standard in 2014.

Back in 2016, Argentina had finally recovered access to international credit markets after a long legal battle with the "vulture funds" – bondholders who swoop in to buy distressed debt, hold out in the ensuing restructuring process, and then litigate to get better treatment than the restructured bondholders did. By highlighting the failures of the international architecture for resolving sovereign-debt crises, Argentina's travails set the stage for reform. In late 2014, the United Nations General Assembly launched a process to create a formal framework for sovereign-debt restructuring; following an endorsement from the International Capital Markets Association in 2014, CACs would henceforth bind minorities to the decisions of qualified majorities.

Argentina borrowed some $42 billion under this new dispensation. But in 2018, market expectations about its prospects changed, triggering a deep, prolonged currency crisis that eventually rendered the country's foreign-currency-denominated public debt unsustainable. Argentina turned to the International Monetary Fund, which provided an unprecedented $57 billion loan, presumably in the belief that the country was facing only a temporary liquidity crisis.

To others, however, it was clear that Argentina was confronting a more fundamental problem of ▶

> By highlighting the failures of the international architecture for resolving sovereign-debt crises, Argentina's travails set the stage for reform."

macroeconomic inconsistency and debt unsustainability. Hence, when the current government – in which I serve as economy minister – took office in December 2019, we immediately initiated a sovereign-debt restructuring to restore debt to a sustainable level, and thus to enable an eventual economic recovery. To that end, the National Congress authorized the government to use the central bank's foreign reserves to continue servicing debt payments up to a limit, thereby avoiding a disorderly default while we conducted the restructuring.

One of the first steps in this process was to work with the IMF to define the terms of debt sustainability – that is, how much debt the country could reasonably afford to service without incurring unacceptable costs, such as a marked increase in poverty or unemployment. In the

The negotiation process was conducted almost entirely via Zoom."

event, we and the Fund's mission to the country each produced analyses that were remarkably similar in their assessment of the relief that would be needed to restore debt sustainability.

We then launched formal negotiations with the country's bondholders on the basis of these pre-pandemic assessments. But, within days, COVID-19 struck Argentina, forcing a massive and rapid mobilization, as well as far-reaching logistical adaptations. The negotiation process was conducted almost entirely via Zoom. And after a few months of intense talks, Argentina and its creditors reached a deal.

The negotiated agreements will save Argentina more than $37 billion in debt payments over the next decade, by lowering the average coupon rate (in US dollars) from about 7% to almost 3%. Moreover, due to the

▲ NURSES DEMONSTRATE FOR HIGHER WAGES AND IMPROVED WORKING CONDITIONS IN BUENOS AIRES.

activation of collective action clauses, the share of restructured debt was expanded from a high acceptance rate of 93.5% to 99% – and to 100% for the stock of bonds that had been issued under the post-2014 CACs.

This process has yielded several lessons for future sovereign-debt restructurings. First, the IMF's role – whether it is positive or negative – absolutely matters. There is widespread recognition among analysts that the Fund has often delayed and undercut restructurings over the past four decades; this time, its contributions helped to restore debt sustainability.

Second, enhanced CACs certainly help, but they are not sufficient. Differences of views between creditors and debtors can still lead to protracted resolution processes, and thus to dangerous economic and social consequences. To complement the new CACs, we must improve the international architecture for sovereign-debt restructuring (a task that the G20 has taken on in the context of the pandemic).

Third, not even improved frameworks can overcome unresolved problems in a country's political economy. Private creditors remain powerful, and can marshal intense lobbying pressure to secure their own interests. Their efforts can be especially effective at undermining the efforts and legitimacy not only of government authorities but even of IMF officials.

> As matters stand, the pandemic will likely leave several other countries with distressed debt that will have to be resolved to secure an economic recovery. "

◢ MARTÍN GUZMÁN.

That said, Argentina's 2020 restructuring benefited widespread support from highly influential global players. In addition to the IMF, 150 internationally renowned academics (including several Nobel laureates), members of the G20, and Pope Francis all endorsed the process. There was widespread domestic support, too, with the National Congress quickly passing two laws that were critical for conducting an orderly restructuring.

As matters stand, the pandemic will likely leave several other countries with distressed debt that will have to be resolved to secure an economic recovery. But many of these countries will lack the Argentine government's capacity to ensure a level playing field for negotiations. In the usual context of asymmetric power, these governments will face creditors' unreasonable demands. They will have to stand firm to defend the interests of the people they represent. To give them a fighting chance, we must institute an international framework to mitigate the imbalances of economic power that so often leave indebted countries worse off. **PS**

Martín Guzmán *is the Minister of Economy of Argentina.*

$37bn

TOTAL DEBT PAYMENTS THAT NEGOTIATED AGREEMENTS WILL SAVE ARGENTINA OVER THE NEXT DECADE.

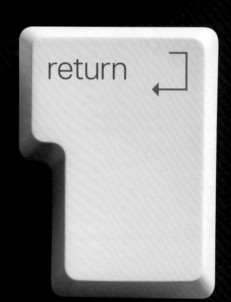

The Pandemic of Fear

Getting Back on the Paris Climate Track

LAURENCE TUBIANA

CEO of the European Climate Foundation

When representatives from nearly 200 countries finalized the Paris climate agreement on December 12, 2015, there were celebrations around the world. But it has now been five years, and the world is in a state of deepening uncertainty. The COVID-19 crisis admits of no quick fixes. The pandemic has ushered in deepening economic and social crises, as well as a wave of increased indebtedness. The geopolitical landscape is as fractured as it has been in decades, and with global supply chains being reorganized, the prospects for achieving deeper global integration through trade are fading.

YET DESPITE ALL THE RECENT TURMOIL, one certainty remains: the climate crisis and the need to stick with the Paris accord, which is the only roadmap that we have for decarbonizing the global economy. Though the agreement initially met with doubts, its primary mechanisms are proving their efficiency and efficacy, and its target of reaching net zero greenhouse-gas emissions by mid-century is now the point of reference for governments and businesses around the world. A growing number of economic sectors – public and private finance, energy, transport, and, increasingly, industry – are setting targets consistent with this objective.

With the 2021 United Nations Climate Change Conference (COP26) approaching, the immediate task for governments is to strengthen their climate plans (following the logic of the Paris agreement's "ratchet mechanism") to lock in emissions-reduction targets for 2030. Politically, the world has reached a tipping point. Donald Trump's infamous June 2017 Rose Garden speech announcing America's withdrawal from the Paris agreement set off a negative domino effect, encouraging Brazil, Australia, and Mexico also to temper their climate ambitions. But now, we are on the cusp of a positive domino effect, as more governments and sectors realize that decarbonization is the key to future economic competitiveness.

In 2020, ambitious new net-zero commitments by China, Japan, South Korea, and the European Union were followed by Joe Biden's election to the US presidency, together marking a decisive shift in the global calculus. In 2021, the G7 and the G20 could both make climate policymaking (not least green finance) the central issue on the global agenda. A majority of members in each group have already established net-zero targets, and thus will need to increase their 2030 benchmarks accordingly. The EU, for example, will need to reduce net emissions by 55% by 2030 in order to meet its 2050 goal.

Beyond the latest developments in the US, the EU, and China, broader economic trends and the mobilization of non-state actors have lent further momentum to climate action. Since 2015, there has been a 22,000% increase in assets committed to fossil-fuel divestments, and many large multinational companies have ▶

Far from being just words on paper, net-zero commitments are having a significant effect on the real economy."

22,000%

THE INCREASE IN FOSSIL-FUEL ASSETS COMMITTED TO DIVESTMENT SINCE 2015.

committed to emissions reductions in line with the Paris agreement.

For example, just in late 2020, Malaysia's state energy giant Petronas joined BP, Shell, and Equinor in setting a 2050 net-zero emissions target, and Spain's Iberdrola, the world's third-largest utility, announced that it will invest €75 billion ($89 billion) over the next five years to double its renewable-energy capacity. Meanwhile, Volkswagen's CEO has acknowledged that the company's survival depends on its ability to pivot to electric-vehicle production, starting with a €33 billion investment between now and 2024.

Moreover, cities, regions, companies, and financial institutions are increasingly working together on climate action, implying that some countries could exceed their national climate goals, while others – such as Brazil and the US – get back on track. These efforts are all underpinned by strong grassroots support for climate action. Even amid a pandemic, polls show that people are as concerned as ever about climate change, and want their governments to do more to protect the planet.

These pressures are creating a virtuous circle. Far from being just words on paper, net-zero commitments are having a significant effect on the real economy. A major trade deal between the EU and Mercosur (Argentina, Brazil, Paraguay, and Uruguay), for example, has been blocked by a number of EU member states over concerns about Brazilian President Jair Bolsonaro's disregard for environmental protections and issues like deforestation. As a result, many Brazilian businesses – including in the beef and soy industries – have been pressuring the Bolsonaro government to change course.

Moreover, in pursuing the European Green Deal, the EU is considering a carbon border adjustment mechanism to put a carbon price on certain imports from outside the bloc. The mechanism will be developed through close engagement with trade partners, and could be the beginning of a new era of cooperation, because other countries committed to net-zero targets will have to push their own industries to pursue decarbonization.

Still, we cannot be blindly optimistic. The fact is that we are running out of time. We know that 2010-20 was the hottest period on record, and that atmospheric concentrations of GHGs have continued to rise fast. We know that emissions from fossil fuels and forest fires reached an all-time high in 2019, and we are now regularly confronted with images of melting glaciers, burning rainforests, streets choked with smog, and small islands battered by superstorms. Even in regions or countries where emissions have peaked, the effort to get to net zero by 2050 will need to be stepped up threefold. Other regions, meanwhile, are not even close to meeting the challenge.

With entire economies and societies changing fast, this is the moment for political leadership to push things across the finish line. The new Biden administration will play a critical part in the global response, but the US alone will not solve the problem. In these times of increasingly distributed global leadership, we all must work together. The international community's next milestones – at the G7, the G20, and COP26 – will be decisive. This is a game of dominoes that we can win. **PS**

Laurence Tubiana, a former French ambassador to the United Nations Framework Convention on Climate Change, is CEO of the European Climate Foundation and a professor at Sciences Po, Paris.

◥ DEFORESTATION IN THE BRAZILIAN AMAZON.

Who Is Attacking Whom?

MOHAMED ELBARADEI
Nobel Peace Prize laureate

The year 2020 demonstrated, once again, that the relationship between the Western and the Arab and Muslim worlds remains muddled, complicated by lingering memories of colonization, wars, and atrocities that date back to the Crusades and, in modern times, to Algeria's war for independence from France and the recent wars in Afghanistan and Iraq.

IT IS A RELATIONSHIP MARRED BY suspicion, distrust, and resentment on the part of many (if not most) Muslims, as well as many in the West. The thin knowledge that both sides of the relationship have of other cultures doesn't lend itself to mutual understanding – a grim fact that radicals (again, on both sides) cynically exploit.

A plethora of recent initiatives have sought to promote intercultural dialogue and foster deeper understanding between civilizations and cultures, particularly Islam and the West. Regrettably, these efforts, including the establishment in 2005 of the United Nations Alliance of Civilizations, have remained mostly confined to the well-educated, and their efforts have had no impact on ordinary people. On the contrary, an extremist attack or utterance overwhelms such initiatives and reinforces the perception of two antithetical cultures locked in inevitable and immutable conflict. The recent renewed uproar in France over cartoons of the Prophet Muhammad, and the shocking atrocities that followed there, clearly demonstrate the deep cultural divide that continues to roil relations between Islam and the West.

Why have these cartoons deepened this fissure anew? Non-secular Muslims perceived these caricatures in a strictly religious framework, and the resulting anger and indignation spanned the entire Islamic world, from North Africa to Indonesia. Many Muslims regarded the images as another deliberate and vicious Judeo-Christian attack on Islam, a continuation of the Crusades by other means. Why, some ask, are attacks on Islam and its sacred symbols permitted, or even encouraged, while criticizing Israel or Holocaust denial is regarded as anti-Semitic and even punishable by law? Likewise, why are the French flag and national anthem protected against desecration, while the most revered symbol of the Islamic faith is not?

Many in the West, on the other hand, regarded the beheadings in France, and previous and subsequent barbaric killings of innocent civilians in European cities, as outright assaults by "Islamist terrorists" against Western culture and the West's way of life. These infamies, they say, were an attack on the West's defining values and freedoms. In the wake of these attacks, public awareness of the depth of the cartoons' offensiveness has diminished.

With French President Emmanuel Macron at the forefront, Western leaders have argued for a strong and unwavering response to the recent murders in France. Even though the overwhelming majority of Muslims have always denied that murderous extremists represent their faith, these tragic events became yet another opportunity for some on both sides to score political points and promote their own narrow agendas. While some opined that Islam needs reform, others claimed that the solution is to restrict Muslim immigration to Europe – a course of action trumpeted most loudly, unsurprisingly, by US President Donald Trump's administration. And some Muslims, in response, want all Muslims to hark back to the Caliphate, a time when the Islamic world was united and powerful.

The truth is that the two cultures have profound philosophical differences regarding the meaning and scope of freedom of expression and belief. Secular Western culture has an expansive view of these freedoms, regarding them as ultimate guarantees against oppression and authoritarianism. The West thus gives precedence to freedom of expression over the sanctity of religious beliefs, regarding the latter as ideas that, like any other idea, should be open to criticism and even derision.

Islamic culture, by contrast, regards religious beliefs as sacrosanct and above the temporal fray, and considers mockery of any Abrahamic religious belief or symbol to be an attack against everything that Muslims hold sacred. The difficult ongoing

> Given all the upheaval, confusion, and polarization in the world today, the last thing that either Islamic or Western civilization needs are new reasons for division and conflict."

political and social transitions in much of the Islamic world mean that many Muslims feel the need to rely even more on the certainties of their faith as a counterweight to the rapid changes in the world. They are not willing to tolerate an attack on the one constant in their lives that gives them solace, hope, and true meaning.

Given all the upheaval, confusion, and polarization in the world today, the last thing that either Islamic or Western civilization needs are new reasons for division and conflict. What is badly needed, instead, is a wide-ranging dialogue between the two cultures that puts all contentious issues on the table, with the hope of gaining a sympathetic understanding of the other's perspective and thus narrowing the gap that exists between both. Whatever the ultimate outcome, the goal on both sides must be to agree on some formula of mutual respect and self-restraint that takes into account each culture's particular sensitivities.

But for any dialogue to succeed, it must confront head-on the larger issue underlying the recent crisis: the distrust that exists between the two cultures. The discussion

should therefore take place at the grass roots and not be limited to the elite. And it should frame intercultural engagement not as an inevitable clash of civilizations, but as an indispensable opportunity to seek mutual accommodation. Only with this shift in perception and mindset will it be possible to build a genuine partnership of equals between Islam and the West. **PS**

Mohamed ElBaradei is a Nobel Peace Prize laureate.

Latin America's Pandemic of Woe

MAURICIO CÁRDENAS

Former Colombian Minister of Finance

EDUARDO LEVY YEYATI

Dean of the School of Government at Universidad Torcuato Di Tella

ANDRÉS VELASCO

Dean of the School of Public Policy at the LSE

Many regions performed badly when confronted with COVID-19, but Latin America fared worse than most, in terms of both lives and livelihoods lost. As of November 2020, nine of the 20 countries with the highest number of COVID-19 deaths per capita were in Latin America. The International Monetary Fund expected the region's output to drop by 8.1% in 2020, with only the eurozone suffering a bigger regional decline. As a result, almost 15 million more Latin Americans will live in extreme poverty.

THE FIRST EXPLANATION FOR THE region's underperformance that comes to mind is poor leadership. Brazilian President Jair Bolsonaro initially claimed that the pandemic was a media trick. Mexican President Andrés Manuel López Obrador denied for weeks that the coronavirus was a threat and continued to hug and shake hands with supporters, only to reverse course suddenly and impose a strict lockdown. But even in those countries that acted early, containment measures were ineffective at reducing the number of COVID-19 cases. Argentina and Peru, which locked down hard, and Chile and Colombia, which followed a more flexible approach, ultimately suffered similarly dismal health outcomes.

That was partly because Latin America's starting point was far from ideal. Too many people had pre-existing health problems, and the prevalence of multigenerational living arrangements facilitated contagion and infection of those most at risk. Large informal labor markets made lockdowns hard to enforce. A high incidence of face-to-face jobs, including in retail sales, and a scarcity of remote work opportunities (owing to poor connectivity and low digital literacy) didn't help, either. Government ineffectiveness left health systems unprepared, despite early lockdowns that postponed the contagion peak.

None of this excuses the fact that many policymakers did too little, too late, but it helps to explain why different strategies yielded similar outcomes. The performance of Uruguay, the region's sole success story, arguably shows what a combination of universal health-care access, greater labor-market formality and social protection, relatively strong state capacity, and sensible leadership might have delivered for all of Latin America.

Economic Shock

COVID-19 inflicted substantial economic damage on Latin America – not least because the region suffered five synchronous blows. Aside from the initial health shock, economies were hit by a decline in commodity prices, a huge drop in export volumes, loss of remittances and tourism revenue, and unprecedented capital outflows early in the crisis. ▶

> Latin America's underperformance during the pandemic has revealed pervasive shortcomings in state capacity that extend far beyond the region's obviously weak health systems."

As a result, many large and small firms ran out of cash and had to close down.

China's quick economic recovery has since boosted commodity prices, and remittances have picked up, too. But the picture for capital flows remains mixed: While Latin America managed to avoid a lasting panic, private outflows often offset the inflows from issuing government bonds abroad. Mexico likely ran a current-account surplus in 2020, with South America as a whole being close to balance, suggesting that external financing conditions remain tight.

This current-account performance also indicates that Latin American governments' countercyclical fiscal spending was insufficient to offset the drop in private consumption and investment. Whereas governments in advanced economies deployed a broad array of discretionary fiscal measures amounting to 20% of GDP, the International Monetary Fund puts the corresponding figure in Latin America at 7%. Only four countries (Peru, Brazil, Chile, and Bolivia) had packages totaling 10% or more of GDP – and this figure includes loans and deferred taxes, in addition to extra public expenditure. Some countries, like Mexico, could have spent more but chose not to, while many others lacked fiscal space or were unable to tap capital markets at reasonable rates.

Latin America's jobs outlook is also discouraging. Despite government furlough schemes that are still funding temporary employment suspensions and mitigating the destruction of salaried jobs, employment has declined by 10–25% (in Lima, an extreme case, it fell by more than 50% in June 2020). As of September, the region's employed population had fallen by more than 25.3 million since the start of the pandemic, with women and young people disproportionately affected. Those under the age of 24 have suffered the greatest employment losses, ranging from 5% in Mexico to 44.4% in Chile.

Moreover, there will be no "back to normal" after the pandemic. Digitalization will likely depress demand for contact-intensive occupations and push firms to automate and streamline their operations at the expense of jobs.

Fragile Structures

Overall, Latin America's underperformance during the pandemic has revealed pervasive shortcomings in state capacity that extend far beyond the region's obviously weak health systems. A few governments lacked the necessary information to identify poor households and provide them with financial help; others had it, but could only write a check instead of transferring funds electronically. The resulting queues and clusters of people outside bank branches may have contributed to the virus's spread. And long after schools reopened in Europe and Asia, classes in much of Latin America remained suspended, owing to persistent logistical difficulties. This is adding permanent knowhow costs to the ongoing job destruction – particularly for low-income households.

Another structural weakness is Latin America's dual labor market, which disproportionately exposes low-income workers to income shocks. About half of the region's workers are informal wage-earners or self-employed without a college degree; in Bolivia, Nicaragua, Paraguay, and

 BURIAL OF COVID
VICTIMS IN CHILE.

Peru, more than two-thirds of workers are informal. Unable to benefit from wage subsidies and furlough schemes, many of them depended during lockdowns on government cash transfers that compensated for only part of their lost income.

In contrast, many Latin American countries offer generous labor protections to high-wage salaried workers. Colombia introduced a subsidy equivalent to 40% of the minimum wage for all formal jobs in firms that had experienced revenue losses. Argentina's government went further, doubling severance payments and eventually banning layoffs outright. But such protection goes to a minority of formal employees, while most informal and independent workers remain unprotected. The consequences of this were painfully obvious in the first half of 2020, with incomes of people at the top dropping by much less than those of people at the bottom.

More Trouble Ahead?

The COVID-19 crisis is an opportunity for Latin American governments to strengthen the state, reform

▲ SANITATION WORKERS
IN RIO DE JANEIRO.

dysfunctional labor markets, and accelerate the search for a new social contract. That means rethinking social protection (including by moving toward universal health coverage), reducing barriers to formal employment, and enhancing income stability for independent workers. But the necessary changes are politically difficult. Restructuring government agencies and labor-market rules quickly ruffles the feathers of powerful vested interests, which is why governments of both the right and the left have until now remained on the path of least resistance.

With several Latin American countries scheduled to hold elections in 2021, the crucial question is whether the regional political climate will improve or worsen in the pandemic's aftermath. A crisis can unite citizens. But the pandemic has also sown plenty of divisions: between professionals who can work from home and factory workers who cannot; between vulnerable elderly people and young people who are subject to government restrictions; and between formal workers who receive wage subsidies and the self-employed who have lost all their income.

Latin America's virus contagion curve may be flattening, but its poverty and business bankruptcy curves continue to rise. If the public-health shock is followed by a protracted economic crisis that leaves many people behind, trust in government and institutions will suffer, and politics will become even more fractured. COVID-19 could yet become a pandemic of instability and hopelessness. **PS**

Mauricio Cárdenas, a former finance minister of Colombia, is Visiting Senior Research Scholar at Columbia University's Center on Global Energy Policy.

Eduardo Levy Yeyati, a former chief economist of the Central Bank of Argentina, is Dean of the School of Government at Universidad Torcuato Di Tella, Faculty Director of the Center for Evidence-Based Policy, and a non-resident senior fellow at The Brookings Institution.

Andrés Velasco, a former presidential candidate and finance minister of Chile, is Dean of the School of Public Policy at the London School of Economics and Political Science.

a new year

KLAUS SCHWAB

*Founder and Executive Chairman
of the World Economic Forum*

The Pandemic of Fear

zero

The year ahead could be a historic one – and in a positive way. Seventy-five years after the original "Year Zero" that followed World War II, we once again have a chance to rebuild. The process after 1945 was literal: building anew from the wreckage of war. This time, the focus is on the material world but also on so much more. We must aim for a higher degree of societal sophistication and create a sound basis for the well-being of all people and the planet.

AFTER WWII, WE DEVELOPED A NEW economic philosophy grounded in collaboration and integration, with material well-being as its primary objective. This project gave rise to international organizations such as the World Bank, the International Monetary Fund, and the OECD, as well as the arrangements that would evolve into the World Trade Organization and the European Union. Neoliberalism – a staunch commitment to free markets and limited government – reigned in the West, where it delivered decades of prosperity and progress.

But this model has broken down. While COVID-19 delivered the final blow, it has been clear for at least two decades that the post-war model is no longer sustainable, environmentally or socially (owing to today's sky-high levels of inequality). The English historian Thomas Fuller famously said that "the darkest hour of the night comes just before the dawn." And yet, we cannot simply assume that a better year will follow an annus horribilis that brought the greatest public-health crisis and the steepest recession in a century. We must act to make it so.

I see three pillars to build on. First, 2021 could be the year when we bring COVID-19 under control. If the recently approved vaccines allow us to beat back the pandemic, we should undertake a reckoning of what we have learned from this crisis. Although vaccines can bring stability, they are not a panacea. Like a peace settlement that ends but does not reverse the devastation of war, stopping the pandemic is merely a first step. The greater challenge will be to fix the structural flaws in our systems and institutions, many of which have failed to provide the necessary care and services to all those who need them.

It will be up to all of us to ensure that our social-welfare and health-care systems are made more resilient for the next generation. The pandemic has reminded us that we cannot aim solely for higher GDP and profits, on the assumption that maximizing these indicators automatically redounds to the benefit of society. It doesn't, which is why the coming year must bring a "Great Reset" in how we approach economic growth and governance.

Second, 2021 will be the year when every major government, as well as broad private-sector coalitions, commit to a "net-zero" target for greenhouse-gas (GHG) emissions. This means that, rather being stuck in a race to the bottom and fearing a continuous "free-rider" problem, the world can benefit from a virtuous cycle of decarbonization.

Already, the European Union has agreed to "enshrine 2050 climate-neutrality in law," China has pledged to become "climate-neutral by 2060," and Japan has made a similar pledge for 2050. With Joe Biden having been elected president, the United States is expected to rejoin the Paris climate agreement, and aim for 100% clean energy and net-zero emissions by 2050.

These commitments amount to a historic development. China, Japan, the US, and Europe together account for well over half of all GHG emissions, and over half of global GDP. The targets outlined in the Paris agreement are now eminently achievable on a national and regional level. Moreover, a series of industry and corporate commitments now complements government efforts. Never before has the global climate movement been so large and so concrete.

Finally, 2021 will be the year when companies pivot from a strictly short-term-profit orientation toward strategies focusing more on the long-term viability of their businesses, and on the interests and contributions of all stakeholders. To be sure, business leaders embraced the concept of stakeholder capitalism back in 2019, with the Business Roundtable's pledge and then in the Davos Manifesto of 2020. But they lacked the means to translate these principled commitments into measurable targets and non-financial

> As in the aftermath of WWII, the building blocks are already in place..."

◀ RECONSTRUCTION IN MILAN AFTER WWII.

◤ DAVID ATTENBOROUGH AT THE LAUNCH OF THE UN CLIMATE CHANGE CONFERENCE.

reporting. That is no longer the case today. With the development of clear "Stakeholder Capitalism Metrics" in 2020, all companies have the tools they need to turn environmental, social, and governance commitments into measurable action.

Again, this is a historic breakthrough that will have global ramifications. The Big Four accounting firms – Deloitte, EY, KPMG, and PwC – all contributed to the new metrics, and can now incorporate them into their own yearly reporting on company performance. And they are joined by a host of large financial institutions, from Bank of America to BlackRock, that have been increasingly vocal supporters of stakeholder capitalism.

These three major developments – a renewed focus on public health and resilience, net-zero pledges, and the arrival of Stakeholder Capitalism Metrics – all but ensure that 2021 will be a new "Year Zero." As in the aftermath of WWII, the building blocks are already in place, providing a foundation on which to construct a new era of improved well-being, inclusive economic growth, and climate action. PS

Klaus Schwab, *Founder and Executive Chairman of the World Economic Forum, is the author of* Stakeholder Capitalism: A Global Economy that Works for Progress, People and Planet *(forthcoming in February 2021).*

The World's Opinion Page

Project Syndicate was established in the early 1990s as an initiative to assist newly independent media in post-communist Central and Eastern Europe. Expansion to Western Europe, Africa, Asia, and the Americas quickly followed, as publishers worldwide sought access to the views of leading thinkers and policymakers on the day's most important global issues.

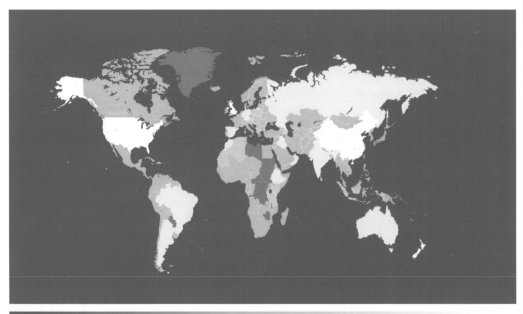

1   PROJECT SYNDICATE'S NETWORK OF MEMBER PUBLICATIONS   13

1,318
WE DISTRIBUTED 1,318 COLUMNS IN 2019.

156
IN 156 COUNTRIES.

590
BY 590 CONTRIBUTORS.

18,716
IN 2019, PS COMMENTARIES WERE PUBLISHED 18,716 TIMES IN OUR MEMBER PUBLICATIONS.

OUR RAPID GROWTH HAS BEEN GUIDED BY RIGOROUS editorial independence and a simple credo: all people – wherever they live, whatever their income, and whatever language they use – deserve equal access to the highest-quality analysis, from a broad range of perspectives, of the events, trends, and forces shaping their lives.

Project Syndicate thus provides an invaluable global public good: ensuring that news media in all countries, regardless of their financial and journalistic resources – and often in challenging political environments – can offer readers original, engaging, and thought-provoking commentary by the world's leading innovators in economics, politics, health, technology, and culture.

Without *Project Syndicate*, most of the publications we serve would be unable to secure comparable content. *Project Syndicate's* unparalleled range and caliber of opinion, our ability to provide analysis of breaking news, and our commitment to focusing minds on complex topics driving the news – development, Asia, Africa, and sustainability, among many others – now benefits some 300 million readers of more than 500 media outlets in 156 countries. **PS**